What School Leaders Need to Know About Digital Technologies and Social Media

Edited by Scott McLeod
and Chris Lehmann

FOREWORD BY DAVID WARLICK

JOSSEY-BASS
A Wiley Imprint
www.josseybass.com

Published by Jossey-Bass
A Wiley Imprint
989 Market Street, San Francisco, CA 94103-1741—www.josseybass.com

Jossey-Bass books and products are available through most bookstores. To contact Jossey-
Bass directly call our Customer Care Department within the U.S. at 800-956-7739, outside
the U.S. at 317-572-3986, or fax 317-572-4002.

Wiley also publishes its books in a variety of electronic formats and by print-on-demand.
Not all content that is available in standard print versions of this book may appear or be
packaged in all book formats. If you have purchased a version of this book that did not
include media that is referenced by or accompanies a standard print version, you may
request this media by visiting http://booksupport.wiley.com. For more information about
Wiley products, visit us www.wiley.com.

Library of Congress Cataloging-in-Publication Data

McLeod, Scott, date.
  What school leaders need to know about digital technologies and social media / edited by
Scott McLeod and Chris Lehmann; foreword by David Warlick.—1st ed.
    p. cm.
  Includes bibliographical references and index.
  ISBN 978-1-118-02224-5 (cloth); ISBN 978-1-118-11670-8 (ebk.);
ISBN 978-1-118-11671-5 (ebk.); ISBN 978-1-118-11672-2 (ebk.)
  1. Educational technology—Planning. 2. Education—Effect of technological
innovations on. 3. Social media. 4. School management and organization.
I. Lehmann, Chris, date. II. Title.
  LB1028.3.M399 2012
  371.33—dc23   2011025366

Printed in the United States of America
FIRST EDITION
HB Printing   10 9 8 7 6 5 4 3 2

To Betsy, Isabel, Lucas, and Colin, who put up with my shenanigans and without whom everything would be meaningless.

—Scott

To my parents, my first and best teachers. To my wife and best friend, Kat. And to the students and teachers of the Science Leadership Academy. You all make the journey so much fun.

—Chris

CONTENTS

FOREWORD

Before embarking on the adventure to which the following pages will transport you, it is important to examine the story that has brought us to this place. I use the term *story* because telling stories is an essential ingredient for successful leadership. In a speech to Pennsylvania superintendents in 2000, cultural anthropologist Jennifer James said that the leaders who incite the transformations in today's teaching and learning will be those who can tell a compelling new story. Dr. James (2000) suggested that this story should have three parts and should do the following:

- Resonate with deeply held values
- Be something that we can point to
- Fit the marketplace

The story that brings us here is about a perfect storm, growing from three converging conditions that are forcing us, for the first time in decades, to rethink education and what it means to be educated in a time of rapid change. We are rethinking the classroom and the definition of teacher, making transparent the boundaries that defined traditional education. We are preparing for a new generation of learners within a new information environment for a future that we cannot clearly describe.

A NEW GENERATION OF LEARNERS

Anyone who has been an educator for more than ten years knows that today's children are different. There is evidence that their brains are physiologically different, elasticity wired in and built from information experiences that are dramatically different from any generation before—experiences that define their culture, which is based on video games, social networking, and a prevailing sense of hyperconnectedness that practically makes the word *good-bye* obsolete. It is an information experience that carries some unique and compelling qualities:

- It is fueled by questions—to overcome built-in barriers.
- It provokes conversation—because it is team-oriented.
- It refines identity—both real and assumed or virtual.
- It is rewarded with currency—gold, coin, attention, powers, and permission.
- It demands personal investment—because there is value.
- It is guided by safely made mistakes—which always add to the player's knowledge.

The foundation of each of these qualities is the responsive nature of children's information experience. Much of what our children do in their outside-the-classroom information experiences is responded to. These responses are often automatic and immediate. But these automatic and immediate responses are not the only form, and perhaps they are not the most powerful. When students are engaged in social networking, the response to their crafted ideas may not come for days or perhaps even weeks after they have posted their thoughts—but when the response comes, it is based on *reading* what was written, not merely *measuring* what was written. The essential qualities of both immediate and delayed responses are relevance and authenticity.

Because such communication is responsive, another defining feature of the experience becomes evident. The players' decisions are constantly being assessed. The report back does not merely identify whether the decision was right (√) or wrong (x).

The return is, "It worked" or "It did not work." Regardless of the response, the learner walks away with a new piece of knowledge.

NEW INFORMATION ENVIRONMENT

Since the 1990s, with the introduction and proliferation of personal computers and the Internet, our information environment has become increasingly networked (accessing our information quickly and globally), digital (machine readable and workable), and abundant (overwhelming). However, the first decade of the twenty-first century has seen another shift in the nature of our information landscape. It has become increasingly participatory and the boundaries that separate author from reader—and producer from viewer—have become fluid. According to a 2007 Pew study, 64 percent of U.S. teenagers have engaged in some form of content creation, up from 57 percent in 2004 (Lenhart, Madden, Smith, & Macgill, 2007).

This dynamic and increasingly accessible global library affords new and empowering learning experiences for our students and it significantly alters the role of the teacher. It also demands a new look at basic literacy, something larger that expands out from basic reading, writing, and numeracy. Today's information landscape requires a wide and exciting range of skills involved in exposing the value of the information we encounter, employing the information by working the numbers that define it, expressing ideas compellingly to produce messages that compete for attention, and habitually considering the ethical implications of our use of information.

AN UNPREDICTABLE FUTURE

By the end of 2010, the amount of information added to the digital universe during the previous four years was more than six times what it was in 2006, from 161 billion gigabytes to 988 billion gigabytes (Gantz, 2007). Information and communication technologies have transitioned from wall-mounted telephones, boom boxes, and bulky television sets to something that we slip in and out of our pockets dozens of times each day. Advances in nanotechnology, biotechnology, and circuit miniaturization promise or threaten to alter our world in ways that even the most knowledgeable among us can barely imagine. We have reached a singularity, of sorts, a place where we educators are challenged to prepare our students for a future that we cannot clearly describe. The education dialogue that we and our communities should be having today is, "What do our children need to be learning today to be ready to succeed, prosper, and seize the opportunities of an unpredictable future—and how do they need to be learning it?"

There is little doubt that at least part of the answer to these questions will be found in the tools and practices that our children have embraced and sometimes have invented for an information landscape that seems set to ignore barriers and empower accomplishment. The following chapters will explore how today's prevailing information environment is already being harnessed to affect the learning experiences that our children need and deserve.

August 2011   David Warlick

Raleigh, North Carolina

References

Gantz, J. (2007, March). *A forecast of worldwide information growth through 2010.* Retrieved from http://www.emc.com/collateral/analyst-reports/expanding-digital-idc-white-paper.pdf

James, J. (2000). *Thinking in the future tense: Leadership for a new age.* New York: Simon & Schuster.

Lenhart, A., Madden, M., Smith, A., & Macgill, A. (2007, December 19). *Teens and social media.* Pew Internet. Retrieved from http://www.pewinternet.org/Reports/2007/Teens-and-Social-Media.aspx

Introduction

Glance at any story about education reform or look over the offerings at most education conferences and you are likely to run across one of the following terms: *Web 2.0*, *twenty-first-century skills*, or *educational technology*. There is near-universal agreement that schools must find ways to transform older teaching practices in order to harness the tools that students have at their disposal today. But for many administrators, trying to figure out the difference among Twitter and Flickr and Moodle and Drupal can leave them wondering where to even begin.

Don't panic. It is nowhere near as hard as you think.

This book, with chapters written by some of the leading experts in the world on educational technology, is meant to introduce you to many of the most useful tools and concepts for an education setting so that you can decide, along with teachers and students and parents, which ones make the most sense for your school.

The contributors hope that this text helps you figure out the often confusing world of social media tools but, more than that, we hope it also serves as an introduction to a set of tools and ideas that have transformed our collective practice as educators. The tools described within, when combined with thoughtful and deliberate pedagogical practice, can create a transformative experience for students and educators alike, and we can no longer imagine teaching without them.

Whether it is the expansion of social networking technologies, the power of digital media creation tools, or the ability to publish to the world instantly, our students and teachers have access to more information than ever before. We all possess the ability to interact with learning networks much wider than at any other time in history. We all now have the unprecedented ability to create powerful artifacts of learning. It is an exciting time to be a teacher and a learner.

We hope this book helps you to enjoy the journey.

The hashtag for this book is #edtechlead
Visit techtoolsforschools.org for additional resources,
interviews with chapter authors, and more!

CHAPTER 1

Blogs

Kristin Hokanson

and Christian Long

What if all teachers and students described their classroom experiences like this (Warlick, 2007)?

> [My students] see themselves as part of a global community—a community that shares. . . . This international audience gives my students a purpose and they are motivated to do their best writing.
>
> *Kathy Cassidy, Teacher, Moose Jaw, Canada*

> I worried about making my students' developing language skills available to a wider audience—but I needn't have. They are developing their own voice and with it a greater degree of responsibility and confidence.
>
> *Paul Harrington, Teacher, Blackwood, United Kingdom*

> We have an authentic global audience for the events that happen in our school. . . . [W]e have a real purpose for writing to inform, to educate, to connect.
>
> *—Teacher from New Zealand*

These comments from educators using Class Blogmeister, a classroom blogging tool developed by David Warlick, show the positive impact that blogs can have on student engagement and performance. *What are blogs and why should educators use them? What does a fully developed blogging project look like and require? Where can educators find blogging resources?* These are some of the questions that educational leaders are asking in order to support twenty-first-century teachers and students.

WHAT ARE BLOGS?

In simple terms, blogs are web-based logs or journals (*web log* shortened to *blog*). The basic concept behind blogging is not new. Social interaction in teaching and learning is a keystone of educational theory. When teachers and students blog, they are able to actively engage audiences outside the usual classroom time boundaries.

Individuals and groups are drawn to blogs for the following reasons:

- They are simple to set up, edit, and publish; no computer language is needed.
- Topics can be as formal or personal as deemed appropriate by the writer.
- Recent entries (*posts*) are easily located as blogs are published in reverse chronological order.
- There are easy ways to subscribe (see Chapter Four).
- Comments from an audience are a standard part of the process, thus creating two-way conversations.

So what are the implications for blogging as pedagogy and what is their potential impact on student engagement?

EDUCATIONAL RATIONALE FOR BLOGGING

SupportBlogging.com, a site set up to help promote an understanding of the benefits of educational blogging, suggests that "one of the great educational benefits of the read/write web, and blogging particularly, is the opportunity for the student to become a 'teacher' by presenting material to an audience. When we teach, we learn" (Hargadon, 2009).

In the past, when a student wrote in class for a single teacher who provided grade-based criticism, student audience was minimal. When student writing was shared or published outside the classroom, feedback also was limited to local, rather than global, area connections.

With the rapid growth of the read-write web, it is as easy to create and exchange content as it is to consume it. Likewise, it is increasingly easy to build an interactive network. With a single click of the mouse, classes can engage in conversations with people from around the world and get authentic feedback. Different than simply keeping a notebook or diary of writing for a single audience, blogs can be public, commented on, and safely moderated before comments are published. This means that educators can provide authentic opportunities for their students to simultaneously analyze, evaluate, and create content that is immediately published for a global audience. Blogging provides new opportunities to receive feedback and see things in a different way. When put to use in education, blogging can have a profound effect on learners.

BLOGGING BEST PRACTICES: THE ALICE PROJECT

"Would you tell me, please, which way I ought to go from here?" [asked Alice]

"That depends a good deal on where you want to get to," said the Cat.

"I don't much care where—" said Alice.

"Then it doesn't matter which way you go," said the Cat.

"—so long as I get somewhere," Alice added as an explanation.

Lewis Carroll, Alice's Adventures in Wonderland *(1865/2008)*

In fall 2009, educator Christian Long's Alice Project (2009) challenged sixty tenth-grade high school students to answer the following questions:

- How can we make *Alice's Adventures in Wonderland* come alive for us?

- More important, how can we create something together that would give an audience outside our classroom its own version of Alice's unexpected journey through Wonderland?

- Can we become the world's most passionate authorities on Carroll's story in the process?

- And how would we create and nurture an equally passionate audience in just two short months?

On a traditional level, the challenges were simple:

- Read a richly annotated version of Lewis Carroll's classic children's story, *Alice's Adventures in Wonderland.*

- Write rigorously about what caught one's eye along the way, balancing playful curiosity with line-by-line analysis.

- Make it interesting for others.

The last challenge, as much as anything else, became the heart of this project.

Students were excited to share their ideas with and get insight from people around the world. The blog was the right "tool" to provide a balance between traditional writing and global conversation. Beyond these questions, the students were required to collaborate on project guidelines, craft and nurture an audience over time, and engage professional judges from around the world to evaluate their individual efforts and teamwork.

TECHNICAL STEPS

The story of Alice is simple enough for a ten-year-old child to appreciate. However, the seemingly limitless intellectual word games and social innuendos in Carroll's work invite a rethink about how students could analyze Wonderland. It demands a more public, question-filled, and debate-centered, writing-as-exploration process. The question was not *if* blogging could work but *how* it should be done to ensure the richest experience possible for students.

It seemed logical to create a series of team-managed blogs to frame student analysis. Additionally, the blog entries were to create ongoing conversations while simultaneously engaging a global audience from day one.

To truly mirror the upside-down experience of young Alice, the students were challenged to be very public about their emerging insights and wrong turns alike. This was not about perfection. It was about fostering conversation. And it was about extending the four walls of the classroom in ways impossible traditionally.

FRAMING THE PROCESS

The first step was creating a teacher-managed home blog to serve as collective archive and one-stop map for visitors. Then a unique Alice Project blog was established for each team to design, compose, edit, and publish. Although there were many free platforms (e.g., Blogger.com or Edublogs.com) that could have been used, the Alice Project used WordPress.com, a free and easy-to-manage blogging system. Nothing was made permanently public until each team's editor had read over posts and comments, followed by the teacher's own review. This allowed classroom flexibility along with appropriate checks and balances.

To establish an audience, thirty-five judges from four continents were brought together to evaluate student work from day one. The judges were assigned specific teams to evaluate in terms of the quality of writing and technology use. Twitter was used to share student progress to thousands of educators around the world. This led to regular blog visitors and comments. Student grades also were based on the quantity and quality of blog posts and comments left on their peers' blogs. Comments from around the world acted as regular criticism and advice to student writers. Feedback was constant and authentic at all points.

REFLECTING ON TIME
SPENT IN BLOGGING WONDERLAND

Here are some of the students' reflections on the Alice Project:

> At first when this project was assigned I thought, "Mr. Long is crazy!!!" . . . I now see that one would have to put in the amount of time and effort to truly experience what this project was about.
>
> Throughout the length of the Alice Project . . . I spent more and more time . . . refining my entries and making them valuable to myself, my group, and the rest of the world.
>
> This was really out of my comfort zone, as in types of schoolwork. I don't want an A just because I participated, but because I actually immersed myself into it and gave it my best shot, even though I didn't know what I was getting myself into.
>
> The attention [our blog] drew really shocked me and allowed me to realize that we made an impact on [an] intellectual society. . . . Also, the quality of work and skill shown by my teammates surprised me. The difference between hearing them speak and seeing what they wrote was incredible. I was humbled by the extent of language skill they had. (Long, 2009)

By the time six weeks had passed, the sixty students collectively had produced 335,000 words and 779 multiparagraph blog entries, wrote 1,200 comments to each other, and received evaluative feedback from a global audience. (See the whole project at http://aliceproject.wordpress.com.)

Most tellingly, the students asked their teacher on the project's completion, "How do we go back and do *normal* school now?"

OTHER EXAMPLES OF BLOGS IN PRACTICE

Obviously not all blogging projects need to have the depth or complexity of the Alice Project, but any opportunities for blogging can be engaging and motivating. Blogs can facilitate inquiry and differentiated instruction by allowing students to explore and contribute to topics that interest them. Blogs support reflection in a public forum while students begin to consider issues such as audience, purpose, bias, and the reliability of information in the digital age.

There are many reasons to engage in blogging in a school setting. Here are some examples of educators' blogging experiences:

- Maria Knee, a kindergarten teacher at Deerfield Community School in Deerfield, New Hampshire, and winner of the 2008 Kay L. Bitter Vision Award for Excellence in Technology-Based PK–2 Education, uses a blog as an interactive showcase of her students' work (http://www.mariaknee.com).

- Dan Meyer, a high school math teacher and Google Fellow currently studying at Stanford University on a doctoral fellowship, uses his blog to bring transparency to his teaching practice (http://blog.mrmeyer.com).

- Jim Gates, a retired Pennsylvania educator, uses his "Tipline" to share ways technology can enhance teaching and learning and examine the real purpose of schools (http://tipline.blogspot.com).

- Anne Smith, an English teacher from Arapahoe High School in Colorado, uses her class blog to post homework assignments, key events, and discussion questions (www .blogger.com/profile/00573450327737964454). This allows other teachers and administrators to visit her classroom to learn from and participate in her lessons. She has created a number of transparent learning experiences using blogs (http://learningandlaptops.blogspot.com), including inviting Dan Pink, author of *A Whole New Mind* (2006), to collaborate on a live blogging project.

- Many instructional leaders are sharing their ideas and thoughts about education in a collaborative group blog *by* school leaders *for* school leaders. Hosted by *Education Week*, the LeaderTalk blog (http://blogs.edweek.org/edweek/ LeaderTalk) expresses the voice of the administrator and provides a great example of best practices by instructional leaders.

RESPONSIBLE BLOGGING

Although blogging comes with many educational benefits, it is not free from its share of issues, including legal concerns that may arise from students facing the public, educators' sharing of their thoughts and practices, copyright issues, and exposure to or interactions with external actors. Many district acceptable use policies (AUPs) have not caught up with the tools that are being used in schools, so it is important that guidelines are clearly set and modeled. Here are some places that you can start to look for resources.

In 2005 Bud Hunt, an instructional technologist for the St. Vrain Valley School District in northern Colorado, started a wiki to provide educators with a collaborative forum for developing guidelines for their blogging practices (http://budtheteacher .com/wiki). The space includes sample AUPs that can be revised for different levels. Many blogging educators use Arapahoe (Colorado) High School's blogging policy (http://ahsblogpolicy .pbworks.com), which describes safe and responsible blogging as well as the traits of successful bloggers to help define general guidelines for the use of blogs. In addition, David Warlick offers an impressive collection of resources for developing schoolwide AUPs (http://landmark-project.com/aup20/pmwiki .php?n=Main .AUPGuides). It is important to remember that rules and regulations in online communications are just as important as classroom rules and procedures.

SUMMARY

Many teachers have discovered the value of classroom blogging as a way to engage students and demonstrate learning in new and transparent ways. Leading in the twenty-first century requires an understanding of the benefits and risks of tools such as blogs. Supporting blogging is one way to provide students with the guidance necessary to use these tools safely, effectively, and ethically.

References

Carroll, L. (2008). *Alice's adventures in wonderland* (p. 33). (Original work published 1865) Retrieved from http://www.gutenberg.org/files/11/11–pdf.pdf

Hargadon, S. (2009, August 14). *Support blogging!* Retrieved from http://supportblogging.com/Educational+Blogging

Long, C. (2009, December 8). *Alice project* blogs. Retrieved from http://aliceproject.wordpress.com/

Pink, D. (2006). *A whole new mind: Why right-brainers will rule the future.* New York: Riverhead Books.

Warlick, D. (2007, June 20). *Warlick's colearners.* Retrieved from http://davidwarlick.com/wiki/pmwiki.php?n=Main .QuotesFromBloggingTeachers

CHAPTER 2

Wikis

Stephanie Sandifer

and Vicki A. Davis

Wikis have been around since the mid-1990s when the first wiki, the WikiWikiWeb, was developed by Ward Cunningham. Cunningham had invented a fast way to edit web pages. As he was pondering what to call his new tool, he happened to travel to a Hawaiian airport where he heard of the "wiki wiki" shuttle (*wiki* is Hawaiian for *fast*). As Wikipedia, the best-known wiki, notes:

> A **wiki** is a website that allows the easy creation and editing of any number of interlinked web pages via a web browser using a simplified markup language or a WYSIWYG text editor. (Wikipedia, 2010)

Wikis are like envelopes for Internet-based information. They can embed just about any other Web-based tool, including uploaded files, images, blog posts, videos, online calendars, Twitter feeds, and much more. Wikis can simplify educators' work by holding common items together without requiring sophisticated programming knowledge. Best of all, there are many sites such as Wikispaces and Wetpaint that offer free wikis to educators.

EDITING WIKIS

When a wiki is created, it often goes through two phases. During the initial phase of content creation, text, files, and other information are added to the wiki. As the next section illustrates, creating and using a wiki is usually fairly simple. This initial phase often is the most labor-intensive, however, as templates are set up and guidelines are drafted. Although it may be tempting to just cut and paste word processing documents into a wiki, educators should be careful to first save them as rich text files (and then copy from those). Otherwise, pasting directly from word processing documents likely will mess up the formatting of the wiki and make the editing process quite frustrating.

After content has been created, a wiki page usually will shift into editing and maintenance mode. This is when administrators will want to check in and make sure that things are being updated and maintained. Otherwise, the wiki becomes just another site that is not maintained properly.

Editing a wiki is not like opening a document in a shared, online word processor. It's usually best for one person to edit a wiki at a time. If live editing by multiple, simultaneous users is required, an online document processing program such as Google Docs may be preferred. If multiple educators will be editing a wiki, it usually is best to have small edits rather than leaving the page open for extended periods of time; otherwise, overlapping edits may conflict with each other. Additionally, the wiki page itself typically should contain only the desired content. Any conversation about the content or potential edits should occur on the discussion tab reserved for that purpose. For those using wikis extensively, it helps to know how to use the wiki history to understand what is happening and to highlight changes made by others.

Despite what some people think, wikis are not always editable by anyone, although that certainly is an option. Wikis can be private, public but only editable by certain people, or editable by the world at large. Each wiki has rules for editing and viewing that are set by the owners. Sometimes wikis are included in website packages or course management software. One of the hallmarks of wikis is that every individual change is recorded, including the identity of the person who made the edit. Wikis thus facilitate the ability of groups to work together collaboratively while still retaining personal accountability, all the way down to the level of an individual comma.

TIPS FOR WORKING WITH WIKIS

Each wiki page includes links for editing, discussions, and reviewing the revision history. The discussion tab provides access to a discussion forum for each page where content creators and editors can discuss the content and the edits. The history tab provides access to a complete history of each page revision. Users can revert to a previous revision to correct editing errors at any point in the development of the wiki. When editing a page, the wiki software allows users to edit using an interface that is very similar to a typical word processor.

WHAT WIKIS MEAN
FOR SCHOOL ORGANIZATIONS

Wikis have the potential to create a paradigm shift in terms of organization and participation. This is crucial in schools that have been striving to become "learning organizations" (Senge, Cambron-McCabe, Lucas, Smith, Dutton, & Kleiner, 2000) but have yet to move away from hierarchical bureaucratic structures. For example, the European investment bank Dresdner Kleinwort Wasserstein experienced a 75 percent drop in e-mail volume and a 50 percent cut in meeting time after wiki use. Implementation of the wiki, which was initially adopted through an informal, grassroots process in the IT department and then spread across the entire company, resulted in greater productivity and more effective organization-wide collaboration (Tapscott & Williams, 2007). In addition to the organizational changes that are enabled by the use of wikis, electronic file storage and e-mail management stresses can be relieved by the reduction in attachments sent back and forth across the organization.

Use of wikis also increases adults' competency with what is now an essential twenty-first-century technology that is increasingly used in the workplace. The U.S. Department of Education (2010) National Education Technology Plan recommends that teachers model "connected teaching" in which "teams of connected educators replace solo practitioners" and in which "connection replaces isolation. Classroom educators are fully connected to learning data and tools for using data; to content, resources, and systems that empower them to create, manage, and assess engaging and relevant learning experiences; and directly to their students in support of learning both inside and outside school."

The wiki is one of the most essential connective technologies and also one of the simplest to use. Additionally, we already are seeing the use of wikilike features in new online software. For example, Google Docs, the free online document processing program from Google, archives changes in a way that allows users to revert to previous versions. This method of storing and tracking changes by user are traditional wiki features that allow for accountability and version tracking as people collaborate. From grant writing to technology or curricular planning, educators no longer have to search for the most recent copy of a file or try to determine who made which changes to a document. Understanding wikis and empowering their use as an administrative team can result in better organizational efficiency and communication.

POTENTIAL USES OF WIKIS

There are a multitude of possible uses for wikis in education.

In the Classroom

Lesson summaries (summarizing lessons learned, often by students)

Notes collaboration (archival record of AP course notes between students or test notes, embedding of video games for studying course content, sharing videos to explain topics)

Concept introduction and exploratory projects (students assigned a topic, research, and edit)

Learn shares (students work in pairs to learn and share with classmates and receive feedback)

Individual assessments and e-folios (collection of content from coursework over a time period)

Rewards (blog or wiki hall of fame, nomination of others for recognition)

Classroom organization (teacher websites, embedding calendars)

In Administration

Collaborative writing (grant writing and management, curricular plans, technology planning, product evaluation)

Meeting planning (agenda development, dissemination of premeeting materials, meeting minutes, action items and reporting)

Reporting (teacher updates, reference materials)

Professional development (professional learning communities, critical friends groups, sharing best practices)

Documentation (memos, policies and procedures, forms, other documents, curriculum and instruction clearinghouse, how-to)

Coordination (home-school, PTO, event planning and sharing, vendor relations)

WIKIS FOR ADMINISTRATORS

School leadership is complex and demanding. Very few school administrators are successful without good organization skills, effective time management strategies, and effective communication skills. Even with these skills, many school administrators struggle with competing demands for their time, energy, resources, and attention. The skilled and effective implementation of wikis by campus leaders can be critical for anyone seeking a way to work smarter and not harder. Wikis provide educational leaders with easy-to-use tools for archiving work, managing documentation and information, and facilitating effective and efficient team collaboration. Wikis can help create an open and flat organization that is no longer controlled by who is on a distribution list but rather who is participative and collaborative.

WIKIS FOR CLASSROOM PROJECTS

Traditional projects in the classroom often include "group work" that involves three to four students working together on a task. The most common complaint of students and teachers is that often only one or two students do all of the work but the other students in the group also receive credit. When a teacher uses a wiki in the classroom, groups can still work together but the edit history now allows the teacher to see individual student contributions and adjust final grades accordingly. Similarly, if a student does something inappropriate on the wiki, the documented evidence in the edit history allows teachers and administrators to move beyond "he said–she said" scenarios and determine appropriate disciplinary consequences.

Wikis are also the tool of choice for massive global collaborative projects such as the Flat Classroom Project (www.flatclassroomproject .org), a multinational, crosscultural learning project that involves students and educators from all across the planet.

WIKI CASE STUDY

Here is an example of how a group of teachers from one school might make use of a wiki in their own professional development. In this scenario, a team from Central High School attends a national education conference—paid for with school funds—with the expectation that they will bring back and share what they learn with other teachers.

Before Wikis

Individual members of the team take notes in a variety of ways: one uses a laptop, two others use a notebook or a journal, and the last two just take notes on the back of handouts that they get at each session they attend. The team gets together on the last night of the conference to compare notes and discuss ideas for professional development sessions that they can facilitate when they return home. Two months later they meet again to plan the professional development. Some of the team members bring their notes to the meeting and some forget to bring their notes.

After Wikis

The team creates a conference wiki where each educator takes his or her notes live while sitting in individual sessions. One page of the wiki is set up to build the professional development agenda that they will use when they return to campus. They list professional development session proposals on the page so that the team can vote on the most relevant sessions to offer when they return. They meet briefly on their return to campus to discuss logistics, then share the complete agenda with the principal for approval. Two months later they deliver the professional development and share the entire wiki (including all their notes) with the rest of the faculty.

TIPS FOR SUCCESSFUL WIKI IMPLEMENTATION BY ADMINISTRATORS

1. Do provide access to the wiki outside of district or school intranets.

   Adoption will happen more quickly if staff can access the wiki from any location and not just from the office or campus. In order to promote adoption, it should be easily accessible and easy to use. Keep it simple.

2. Do encourage grassroots adoption.

   If your entire organization or school is not yet ready to plunge into systemwide wiki use, allow smaller groups or teams to create their own wikis. Be supportive of these grassroots efforts and highlight their accomplishments when appropriate so that the other staff members become aware of how the wiki use is contributing to the organization.

3. Don't impose an overly strict structure to the wiki.

   Do allow employees to define a structure that meets their needs as often as possible. Start with a skeletal structure and allow employees the flexibility to change that structure as needed. Allow for an organic, flexible, and evolving structure from the beginning of the wiki implementation.

4. Don't block access to free wiki sites such as Wikipedia, PBworks, or Wetpaint.

These free sites offer all staff members an easily accessible and easy-to-use space where they can explore how to use wikis by creating their own for personal use. Access to these wiki sites also allows employees to become exposed to wikis used in other schools and districts, to network with other educators who have adopted wiki use, and to see a wide variety of uses across classrooms, schools, and districts.

5. Do get permission to publish images of students and colleagues.

   This is a no-brainer for legal reasons—especially when students are involved. Some include photo permission forms as part of their admissions packet and have on file permission requests of parents. Additionally, schools should have rules for identification of people in photos. Many schools only allow first names and last initials for privacy reasons.

6. Do praise and encourage *any* participation, then, praise and encourage meaningful participation.

   We all like to receive a pat on the back when we participate in ways that add value to the whole. Public praise and recognition may also send an encouraging message to staff members who have been reluctant to use the wiki in their work.

7. Do insist on real names or a consistent use of a pseudonym for user names. Don't allow for anonymous edits or comments. Do set a positive, constructive tone early.

   Online etiquette is very important because we lose the visual and verbal cues that are present in face-to-face settings. The use of real names (or at least first name and last initial for students) or making sure that a list of pseudonyms and corresponding real names are held by the teacher or administrator helps provide the transparency necessary for safe, positive, and effective online collaboration and it holds people accountable for the content that they create.

8. Do start small and make edits together as a group the first time.

   Group mentoring of new technologies can be as effective as one-on-one mentoring for most users, but, of course, this is even more effective if paired with follow-up mentoring for users who find the wiki challenging. Encourage more tech-savvy users to be bold in their use of the wiki while also acting as mentors to the users who need more help and guidance.

9. Do promote the use of wiki instead of e-mail for projects and tasks that you are designating to be done on the wiki and avoid the temptation to provide information in media other than the wiki.

   Gently remind users to share information through the wiki rather than through e-mail if you are pushing project management to the wiki for a task. Model the use of wiki for collaboration and the use of e-mail for short, immediate messages that do not require intensive collaborative efforts. Do not provide alternative media or locations for information and content that is more appropriate for inclusion on the wiki. When employees ask where they can find that information, remind them that it is on the wiki. The wiki should become the one-stop shop for all your collaborative documentation and information.

10. Do understand that many of your users will not be comfortable with technology.

    Be willing to accept that some of your employees have yet to accept e-mail as the standard form of written communication across your organization. Althbugh you should be aware of this, you should also create opportunities for them to use the wiki with some guided practice.

11. Do let go of the notion that physical presence is the only prerequisite for collaboration and productivity.

These new tools allow for collaboration from anyplace at any time. Time is a scarce resource in our business, and it is frequently very difficult to coordinate face-to-face meeting times and locations with busy leadership teams who are taking care of the important school or district business. Much of our typical brainstorming and collaboration can take place through wikis and other web-based tools.

12. Do provide some one-on-one hand-holding and coaching for users who need it.

One-shot workshops on a professional development day are not effective means for helping faculty learn new technology. Understand that you will have some users who will need some one-on-one time to learn how to use the wiki.

13. Do be patient.

It cannot be stated enough that this process takes time. Be patient with the learning curves of the users, and be patient with each individual's path and pace in learning.

SUMMARY

The uses of wikis by educators are nearly limitless, constrained primarily by the scope of our imaginations. Although many of the uses listed in this chapter relate to collaborative team planning and documentation, wikis can also be used by individuals as personal online notebooks where information can be documented, organized, and archived. This private space for experimentation is one of the best ways to explore and learn about the uses of wikis.

References

Senge, P., Cambron-McCabe, N., Lucas, T., Smith, B., Dutton, J., & Kleiner, A. (2000). *Schools that learn: A fifth discipline fieldbook for educators, parents, and everyone who cares about education.* New York: Doubleday/Currency.

Tapscott, D., & Williams, A. D. (2007, March 27). *The wiki workplace*. Bloomberg Businessweek. Retrieved from www .businessweek.com/innovate/content/mar2007/id20070326_ 237620.htm?chan=search

U.S. Department of Education. (2010). National Education Technology Plan 2010. Retrieved from www.ed.gov/technology/netp-2010

Wikipedia. (2010). *Wiki*. Retrieved from http://en.wikipedia.org/ wiki/Wiki

Suggested Resources

Mader, S. (2008). *Wikipatterns: A practical guide to improving productivity and collaboration in your organization*. Indianapolis: Wiley.

Sandifer, S. (2010). *Wikis for collaboration and communication in schools*. Larchmont, NY: Eye on Education.

Shirky, C. (2008). *Here comes everybody: The power of organizing without organizations*. New York: Penguin Press.

CHAPTER 3

Podcasts and Webinars

Steve Dembo

and Wesley Fryer

Learning in the twenty-first century is changing in basic ways, and the access educators can now enjoy to recorded podcasts as well as live and recorded webinars reflects this basic change in several ways. Traditionally, professional development for educators has taken different forms, but the most predominant models involve face-to-face meetings and reading. Attending a presentation or series of presentations at school during predesignated, districtwide "professional development" days remains common in the United States. Some schools use book studies as a way to refresh and renew educator perspectives on teaching and learning. Although these professional development activities can be beneficial, it is challenging to provide customized, differentiated learning opportunities relevant to individual educators' needs using only these models.

In contrast to traditional professional development, podcasts and webinars offer opportunities for educators to shift the time and place of their learning, listening to, and reflecting on ideas to the schedule and location most convenient for them. Educators can be permitted to self-select topics for their professional development when podcasts and webinars are used. In this chapter, we will define podcasting and webinars in the context of twenty-first-century professional development, explore several outstanding examples of these digital professional learning opportunities, and offer suggestions for ways interested educators can get started using these powerful learning options.

WHAT ARE PODCASTS AND WEBINARS?

Podcasts and webinars are similar but different. This section describes each as well as the differences between the two.

Podcasts

Podcasts are usually audio or video files shared online and subscribable within software called a *podcatcher* or a *podcast client*. iTunes (www.apple.com/itunes) is one of the most popular podcatching software programs, but other options are available (Wikipedia, 2011c). When users subscribe to a podcast channel, included files can be readily downloaded to a computer as well as a mobile learning device such as an iPhone, iPod touch, or iPad.

Podcasts are sometimes called *nonstreamed webcasts* because they are prerecorded and do not require a live Internet connection. One of the most powerful and transformative characteristics of podcasts is this ability to download content and take it on the go using a mobile device.

Webinars

Webinars are webcasts that take place live and require participants to use an Internet-connected computer. Although it is possible for an audience to watch a live webinar together, with a single computer connected live at the front of a classroom, the optimal situation is one in which every participant can log into the webinar directly using his or her own computer. This permits each individual to respond to presenter polls, add feedback as well as questions in the provided text-chat area, and participate directly in discussions using a microphone and webcam if permitted by the webinar administrator.

Although podcasting is intended to be prerecorded and listened to at one's leisure, webinars are primarily a live format. There are many different formats and software for webinars, but the one thing all webinars have in common is that they take place in real time. Invitations are extended in advance and people watch the event as it happens. Most webinar software has some ability to save what has taken place, allowing archives to be created for viewing at a later time. It is not unusual for an event to be broadcast live, recorded, and then released later in a format similar to traditional podcasts. When a webinar is recorded and linked within a web feed for download within a channel of content, that recorded file has technically become a podcast.

BENEFITS FOR PROFESSIONAL DEVELOPMENT

Educators need to be aware of the professional development opportunities available via podcasts and webinars for several reasons.

Free or Inexpensive

Many podcast and webinar options are available today that are either free or very inexpensive. Educational budgets are limited in schools. Administrators are challenged to stretch available money as far as possible, and professional development often is underfunded. By using podcasts and webinars for professional development, educators in large and small schools can enjoy access to innovative, cutting-edge ideas as well as other classroom teachers sharing best practices for free or very little cost.

Differentiated

The best professional learning plan is customized to the individual needs of different people. Whenever large-group instructional methods are employed, differentiation is challenging. By using the diverse menu of professional development for podcasts and webinars available online today, educators and school administrators can provide relevant, specific learning opportunities for themselves as well as colleagues while also meeting individual interests.

Flexible

Because so many different options are available for live webinars and prerecorded podcasts today, educators can use these resources in flexible ways that meet the requirements of different schedules and calendars. Portions of prerecorded podcasts and recorded webinars can be used in face-to-face professional development sessions and followed up with discussions and hands-on practice when appropriate. Educators can listen to podcasts on the go as well as at school. When podcasts are downloaded to a mobile device such as a phone or MP3 player, educators can listen to them like an audiobook on a drive commuting to or from work or on a walk after school at the neighborhood park. Webinars and podcasts can also be used during traditional face-to-face professional development times at school when the budget or schedule does not permit speakers from outside the school to present in person.

PODCAST AND WEBINAR EXAMPLES

A variety of free and inexpensive podcasts as well as webinars are available online that focus specifically on educator professional development topics.

Exemplary Podcasts for Professional Development

Since 2006, the free K12 Online Conference (www.k12online conference.org) has provided ongoing opportunities for educators around the world to teach each other and learn together using both audio and video podcasts. Each year, generally in October, more than forty new presentations are posted to the K12 Online Conference blog and linked within conference podcast channels. Presentations are prerecorded by presenters from around the world and compressed into video as well as audio-only files that can be downloaded using podcast client software or viewed in a web browser. Since 2008, K12 Online Conference presentations also have been published to the video-sharing website dotSUB (www .dotsub.com). dotSUB permits video annotations to be added in multiple languages, making videos more accessible not only to individuals with hearing impairments but also to people who do not understand the native language of a presenter. Conference podcast feeds for past years are available at the K12 Online website.

In the first four years of the conference, separate audio and video podcast channels were created for K12 Online Conference presentations. Starting in 2010, an iTunes U channel was created for K12 Online thanks to the Arizona State Department of Education, Arizona State University, the IDEAL Community, and the Arizona Applied Learning Technologies Institute. Content available in iTunes U is only downloadable using iTunes software unless links to media files linked outside of iTunes U are provided separately. iTunes U (www.apple.com/education/itunesu) was announced by Apple in May 2007 and provides access to thousands of recorded lectures, lab demonstrations, language lessons, and other recorded video as well as audio files (Wikipedia, 2011a). Some universities and university projects, such as MIT Open Courseware (http://ocw.mit.edu/index.htm), provide podcast files in iTunes U and on publicly accessible websites.

The slogan for iTunes U is "Learn anything, anytime, anywhere." That phrase summarizes the philosophy of many educators embracing podcasting for professional development. The diverse array of available podcasts, combined with the ability to take these media files on the go in the car, in the classroom, or on a walk, make podcasting an extremely powerful and flexible way to learn professionally.

Exemplary Webinars for Professional Development

A variety of organizations and institutions now offer webinars for free as well as on fee-based schedules. Two of the best providers of educational webinars today are Classroom 2.0 Live (http://live .classroom20.com/) and The Discovery Education Network (DEN) (http://blog.discoveryeducation.com/blog/category/webinars).

Classroom 2.0 Live is sponsored by Elluminate (a commercial provider for webinars found at www.elluminate.com) and provides weekly webinars addressing a wide variety of educational topics. Because Classroom 2.0 Live programs are on a regular schedule (every Saturday) and start at a consistent time (9 AM Pacific; 12 PM Eastern), it is easier for educators to plan for and join these events. More information about Classroom 2.0 Live is available at http:// live.classroom20.com.

Regular webcasts by educators for educators also are provided on EdTechTalk (www.edtechtalk.com). EdTechTalk is a "collaborative, open webcasting community" in which educators are empowered to teach with and learn from each other using live shows broadcasted over the Internet. A variety of regular programs are hosted by EdTechTalk focusing not only on educational technology topics but also on many other ideas related to classroom learning and teaching. Some of the regular programs on EdTechTalk include Seedlings, EdTechBrainstorm, Parents as Partners, Teachers Teaching Teachers, Women of Web 3.0, and the K12 Online Echo. Participants in EdTechTalk webcasts can use a web browser and headphones (or computer speakers) to participate in these live events.

The Discovery Education Network regularly sponsors free webinars for educators. One example was the October 2010 DEN Fall Virtual Conference (Fall VirtCon). Although the conference is over, sessions were recorded and archived online. These can be downloaded from the DEN website (http://blog.discoveryeducation .com/fall-virtcon-2010) but because sessions are not linked within a web feed or podcast channel they are not technically available as podcasts. DEN-sponsored webinars are offered throughout the year for free and address a variety of educational issues appropriate for formal as well as informal professional development.

GETTING STARTED WITH PODCASTS

To use educational podcasts for professional development, educators must do two things:

- Find an educational podcast that is subscribable or viewable online.
- Download and install podcatcher software (iTunes, Juice, and iPodder are some examples).

Educational podcasts can be found online using a search engine such as Google, but a great way to find podcasts is to use a directory specific to education or with educational categories. The Education Podcast Network (www.epnweb.org) is a website created by David Warlick to showcase examples of education podcasts. Because of the large number of iTunes users today, the iTunes podcast directory for education (including different subcategories) is one of the best ways to find podcasts. iTunes users have opportunities to rate and write reviews of podcasts, and similar podcasts that other people like are displayed within iTunes when viewing a podcast channel.

Although podcasts are often associated with iTunes and Apple, it is important to understand podcasting is not something Apple employees invented or the company owns just because they created iPods. Some webcasters use the term *netcasts* to refer to podcasts, in part due to concerns that the podcast term is associated so strongly with Apple and Apple products (Wikipedia, 2011b). Although recorded audio and video files can and are consumed using a computer web browser, true podcasts or netcasts can be transferred to a mobile media device for consumption on the go. The English Wikipedia includes an extensive list of podcatcher software options (Wikipedia, 2011c) for different computer operating systems. Although it is not technically necessary to download and use specific podcast client software to hear podcasts, these programs not only facilitate rapid downloading of multiple episodes but also permit subscribing so new episodes are automatically downloaded to a computer after they are released, when the podcatching program runs.

GETTING STARTED WITH WEBINARS

Webinars depend on different proprietary, commercial platforms to handle the broadcasting of content and the reception of and interactivity with content by participants. Webinars usually combine presenter narrative with visuals of some sort to create a cohesive presentation. Beyond that, features and interactivity options can be quite varied. Some webinar solutions provide the opportunity for people to use a webcam to display a live video feed of the presenter, "talking head" style. Others offer up a teleconference so that the presenter and attendees can chat with each other, and still others employ the use of VoIP (Voice over Internet Protocol) to facilitate a teleconference-style conversation through computer headsets. For the visuals themselves, the two most frequently used formats are shared slides (PowerPoint and Keynote) or a live demonstration using screen-sharing features. Many webinar platforms provide the ability to display the presenter's screen in real time to the attendees, allowing them to use applications, browse the web, and even share videos.

Given the wide variety of webinar platforms and variations, it may seem a bit daunting to get started with them. However, often the largest obstacle to getting started is not technical, it's mental. Many people find the idea of sharing their information live with other people intimidating and can become nervous, even when they are extremely familiar with the material being presented. Additionally, not being in the same room with the audience and being able to use their body language as a gauge for how the presentation is going can be disconcerting. The only solution for alleviating these stresses is to become familiar with the chosen platform ahead of time, practice with it thoroughly, and dive right in! Nothing cures the intimidation of a new technology like experience.

One of the most attractive aspects of using webinars is that they provide opportunities for presenters to interact with attendees. As mentioned before, many platforms allow the use of teleconference audio or VoIP. This permits the host to converse directly with attendees, not using a shared phone bridge but using participant computers' screens and audio peripherals. Multiple people can be granted permission to talk during a webinar. Although it can be wonderful to hear multiple voices and perspectives, it can also be confusing and distracting if too many people have microphone access during a webinar. When there are only four or five people in a webinar, it is easy to avoid people stepping on or talking over each other. When there are more than twenty people attending, it can be much more challenging due to the potential for distractions via background noise. Because of this, many webinar platforms offer a chat window for attendees to communicate through. Questions and answers can be asked there without interrupting the audio of the primary presentation, and can be addressed later in the session.

An additional benefit of a webinar's chat window is that it can serve as a backchannel (an online discussion area for participants that exists parallel to the presentation being delivered) for attendees. The very idea of a backchannel is representative of the perceptual shift we are experiencing in the twenty-first century. New collaboration tools have allowed people to begin reflecting and synthesizing information as a group, in real time. Instead of just being a way to communicate with the presenter, the chat window has become a way for attendees to contribute to the presentation itself. As information is being presented, the audience can share their thoughts, connections, and links to related material. Some people document key points from the presenter and others may use the chat to challenge those same points. Either way, the use of the backchannel to transform passive attendees to active contributors is similar to the same shift educators are seeking to facilitate in their own brick-and-mortar classrooms.

Within schools, webinars can be a very effective method of providing professional development and training. Because the only requirement to attend is an Internet-connected computer, individuals can participate from home or school, without the complexity of organizing face-to-face meetings. Because the event can be recorded and made available later, it is ideal for communicating technical processes that everyone is required to know. Those who might need additional support can be encouraged to attend in real time and have their questions answered by the presenter. Those who are unable to attend live will have the recorded version available to them to reference when it is more convenient. It can be a fantastic way to share changes to the computer system, new software that is available, or how to make use of new technologies available to teachers. However, it can also be a cost-effective means for communicating with the parent community. For example, districts could host a series of guest speakers to share information about cyberbullying and digital citizenship. Parents could attend from the comfort of their own homes and still have the chance to have their individual questions answered by an expert. The entire series could be archived and made available via DVD for any parents who may not have an Internet connection in the home.

A variety of different webinar platforms are available today. Unless you're hosting the webinar yourself, you will not have a choice about the platform used. Some of the popular platforms in use today include the following:

- Elluminate (www.elluminate.com)
- Adobe Connect (www.adobe.com/products/adobeconnect .html)
- WebEx (www.webex.com)

The English Wikipedia includes a good list of webinar platform options in the article on web conferencing (Wikipedia, 2011d). Although the features of these solutions vary, generally each provides a downloadable client application that webinar attendees can use to listen, watch, and participate in the different elements of a presentation. It's up to the webinar organizers and presenters to decide which of these features to use and make available to participants during the actual presentation.

Get started with webinars by listening to an archived version available online as a recorded video! Find an upcoming webinar using one of the websites we've referenced in this article, which feature regular programs. The best way to understand the power and potential of webinars is by participating in them yourself. If possible, ask a colleague to join you and help troubleshoot any issues that may arise when you attend a live webinar. Take time to reflect, discuss, and share about your webinar experiences with others afterward.

SUMMARY

We learn the most from the company we keep, and the other educators as well as students with whom you work may gain their first exposure to the world of online learning via podcasts and webinars. We encourage you to take the next step and find at least one podcast and one webinar with an appealing topic. Then watch them! We're surrounded by a wealth of good ideas and creative people today in our twenty-first-century-networked environment. Take advantage of these opportunities and share them with others!

References

Wikipedia. (2011a). *iTunes*. http://en.wikipedia.org/wiki/ITunes# iTunesU

Wikipedia. (2011b). *Leo Laporte*. http://en.wikipedia.org/ wiki/Leo_Laporte#Netcasting

Wikipedia. (2011c). *List of podcatchers*. http://en.wikipedia.org/ wiki/List_of_podcatchers

Wikipedia. (2011d). *Web conferencing*. http://en.wikipedia.org/ wiki/Web_conferencing#Software_and_service_providers

CHAPTER 4

RSS and RSS Readers

Will Richardson

and Karl Fisch

What if you could create your own constantly updated newspaper, one in which every story is about a topic you're interested in, one that pulled together the best thinkers, artists, writers, and leading voices around whatever you're passionate about, be it education, organic cooking, or Alaskan fly fishing? What if it was multimedia, filled with relevant photos and videos, and what if it even published every time your school's name was uttered on the web? Best of all, what if all of it—all of the stories, blog posts, search results, videos, and more—came together in that newspaper for free? Would you be interested in reading?

All that and more is easily possible thanks to what might be the best-kept secret in the new learning world: real simple syndication or RSS. A powerful tool that was originally built for blogs, RSS gives us the ability to subscribe (for free) to as many feeds of information as we think we can handle, bringing all the latest news together in one, easy-to-manage spot either online or off. It's as if—in the words of MIT Media Lab founder Nicholas Negroponte (1996)—we were creating a "daily me" (p. 153).

The good news is that RSS is an easy-enough tool to start using right now. The bad news is that you'll quickly discover more great feeds to read than you probably can handle. With almost two billion potential content creators and sharers now hooked into the web, the pool of information is incredibly wide and deep. But efficient use of RSS speaks to one of the key new literacies offered by the National Council of Teachers of English in 2008: we must be able to "manage, analyze, and synthesize multiple streams of simultaneous information" (www.ncte.org/positions/statements/21stcentdefinition). RSS helps us do all of that and more.

GETTING STARTED

To get started, navigate to Google Reader (www.reader.google.com). You'll need to have a Google account to start using Reader, which is probably the easiest of the many RSS *aggregators*, as they are called. When you're logged into Google and you go to your Reader, you'll find an introductory video that will give you a pretty good overview of the tool. You also can find dozens of great how-to videos at YouTube when you do a search for "Google Reader tutorial."

Although there are lots of things you can do with Reader, the most important process centers on finding and subscribing to feeds. Without going too deeply into the technology (which is pretty transparent), almost every blog on the web has an RSS feed built into its code, which means that you can subscribe to just about every one of them. There are a number of ways to subscribe, but here is the most consistently easy method: Once you identify a blog that you want to add to your daily newspaper, simply copy its web address, navigate over to your Reader page, click on the "add subscription" button toward the top left of the page, and paste in the address. Once you click "add," the latest blog posts from the feed you added will show up in the right-hand column.

Adding feeds from newspapers or magazines, from photo or video collections, or from searches on the web are almost as easy.

Say you find a section in the *New York Times* that you want to pull in—or videos on a particular topic on YouTube as identified by the particular keyword or tag that it's been posted with—all you need to do is copy and paste the web address of the section or keyword page into Google Reader. Unfortunately, not every news or website will have an RSS feed available. If that's the case, your Reader will tell you so when you try to subscribe.

A couple of other sites that serve as RSS aggregators are Netvibes (www.netvibes.com) and Pageflakes (www.pageflakes .com). Although Google Reader is purely for your private use (even though you can share with the world certain items that come through your feeds), both of these services make creating public newspapers easy. They are especially useful for educators looking to share specific news or content sources to a classroom or even a faculty group.

RSS FOR PERSONAL LEARNING

Using RSS to learn about whatever your passion is can take many forms, but here are five great ways to start. Each of them can lead to some great connections as you build your own learning community.

1. *Find great bloggers.* At this point, every topic has some really great bloggers out there writing about it, and blogs are the perfect way to start building out your Reader. To see who is writing about your area of interest, do a search at Google's Blog Search page (http://blogsearch.google.com). Just put in your topic of interest and you'll see who's been writing about it. You'll need to take some time to vet the results in terms of topics, writing quality, comments, bias, and so on, but if you find someone who's consistently interesting, subscribe. Then, see who that person reads and you'll find other bloggers who might be worth reading.

2. *Set up a search.* Say you want to track every time your favorite author (or sports team or actress or vacation spot) is mentioned in the blogosphere or in the news. You can actually just do a search at Blog Search or at Google News (http://news.google.com) and then subscribe to the results page (remember, just copy and paste the web address into your Reader). This works with other searches at multimedia sites, for example YouTube or Flickr. Say you want to collect videos or photos of your favorite animal or math concept; just search for the keywords (for example, *persian cat* or *trigonometric identities*) and then subscribe to the results.

3. *Collect bookmarks.* Social bookmarking sites such as Diigo (http://www.diigo.com/) now allow us to share the best websites and resources that we find on the web with the world. And it also allows individuals to subscribe to the bookmarks saved under any given tag. So if you want to add a list of bookmarked sites that others have found around, say, *Spanish* and *lessons* to your Reader, just do the search, and use the address to subscribe. From that point on, you'll get every new bookmark saved with those keywords.

4. *Follow the tweets.* Twitter has become a crucial tool in many educator's learning lives, and you can use RSS to mine out the most relevant tweets and send them to your Reader. The use of hashtags (keywords preceded by the # sign, as in #knitting) in many Twitter updates makes subscribing easy. Go to the Twitter search web page (http://search.twitter.com), enter the hashtag, and subscribe. You also can enter a regular old word such as *literacy* and get notified any time anyone uses the word in a tweet. Obviously, this can quickly get overwhelming, so be careful to what you subscribe. But it also can be a great way of finding and connecting to others who share your interests.

5. *Get the tunes.* iTunes has some great resources in its iTunes U section: course materials, lectures, language lessons, interviews,

and more. You can subscribe to the channel that you want by opening it up in iTunes and right-clicking on the "subscribe" button, copying the link, and adding it to your Reader.

RSS FOR SCHOOL LEADERS

As you've just read, RSS is a great way to further your own personal learning, but how might you begin to use it at school? There are many, many ways to answer that question and new ways come along every day. Let's look at just a small sample to get you started.

Administrators: Reputation Management

Among myriad duties most school administrators have is reputation management, keeping an ear to the ground to stay apprised of issues that concern their school community and intervening when necessary. This is more challenging these days because there are so many additional—and often very public—ways for the community to be having that conversation, and the community that is discussing your school can be so much larger. It's no longer enough to know what's being talked about at the grocery store, at church, and in the local newspaper; administrators also need to stay on top of what's being said on blogs, Twitter, and YouTube (among others).

Search Google News, blogs, Twitter, YouTube, and any other potential sites for the name of your school, then subscribe to the feed for that search in your Reader. You'll then know anytime your school is mentioned. You'll have to experiment with the search terms, depending on the name of your school, and you'll never catch everything that's said, but this is a great way to tap into the larger conversation that's happening around your school. You also may want to subscribe to the changes to your school's Wikipedia page.

Teachers: From PLCs to PLNs

Many schools follow a professional learning community (PLC) model of staff development. RSS allows you to make your PLCs both more effective and more inclusive. Even when schools provide dedicated time for PLCs, it's never enough. If teachers combine blogging with PLCs, then those conversations can continue at times (and locations) that are more convenient to individual teacher's schedules. By collating feeds of individual teachers reflecting on their practice, and of PLC teams reflecting on their progress, everyone in your learning community can engage in deeper and broader discussions of teaching and learning at your school.

Although there are tremendous ideas within your local learning community, there is a larger discussion about these same ideas worldwide. Your teachers can participate in a global PLC—often called a personal learning network (PLN)—of educators and others discussing the areas of teaching and learning about which they are passionate. As teachers discover others who are interested in the same topics, they can build their own PLNs. They can subscribe to blogs, podcasts, and social bookmarks (to name a few); receive a constant stream of thought-provoking ideas and resources; and participate and make their own contributions. Not only will they reap the benefits of tapping into the larger conversation, but they will also model lifelong learning for their students (administrators can participate right alongside teachers).

Students: Bringing It All Together

Everything described in this chapter for educators is even more critical for students. Although administrators are concerned with the reputation of their schools, students need to be curators of their own online, digital footprint. They need to use RSS (among other tools) to monitor, manage, and promote their own digital reputations. The old saying that you never get a second chance to make a good first impression is even more important today because increasingly the first impression our students make on others isn't going to happen face-to-face, it's going to be virtual. RSS provides a means to benefit from and manage digital first impressions.

Although PLNs are a natural extension of the PLC process for educators, they are absolutely essential for students. Students are the ultimate knowledge workers, and PLNs allow them to expand and maximize their learning. They can use RSS on a small scale to help manage group work or individual classes and on a much larger scale, to pursue ideas and conversations around the globe. They can not only tap into the power of global resources for their required assignments but also, perhaps even more important, pursue their own learning passions. Students are no longer constrained in their learning by geography and the interests of their local peers but can join (and co-create) learning communities dedicated to the topics they are interested in. RSS is a gateway to the human network.

GET STARTED

Go to http://reader.google.com and set up Google Reader. If you don't have a Google account, you'll need to create one, but it's free and you're going to want one anyway (check out www.google.com/support/reader/?hl=en for help).

Subscribe to at least three and no more than seven education bloggers. (Yes, those numbers are completely made up but start small.) How do you find them? Well, you can start with various lists online (such as this one: http://movingforward.wikispaces.com/Blogs) or just find one or two bloggers you like (perhaps http://weblogg-ed.com and http://bigthink.com/blogs/dangerously-irrelevant) and follow the links from their posts and from the folks who comment.

Then read. And reflect. And write (comment on others or start your own blog).

Then repeat.

You're on your way.

Resources

Common Craft. (2011). *RSS in plain English*. Retrieved from www
.commoncraft.com/rss_plain_english

Negroponte, N. (1996). *Being digital*. New York: Vintage.

Richardson, W. (2010). *Blogs, wikis, podcasts and other powerful web
tools for classrooms*. Thousand Oaks, CA: Corwin Press.

CHAPTER 5

Digital Video

Mathew Needleman

Many educators are wondering why they would want to integrate video production into their classrooms, reasonably asking what advantages it offers them and their students compared to other options. The short answer is that by creating movies students can participate in a highly engaging medium that has existed for more than one hundred years. The tools for creating movies have become affordable for the average classroom only in the past decade thanks to the rise of digital video cameras and inexpensive video-editing software. Through the use of online video-sharing sites such as YouTube, student work has the potential to gain an audience that extends far beyond the teacher and the four walls of the classroom. This chapter will address some practical considerations for beginning a video production program in a school and provide some specific examples to facilitate curricular idea generation.

The multiple intelligences required to create videos often engage students who are otherwise unengaged and can appeal to learning modalities that otherwise remain untapped in a traditional paper-and-pencil classroom. Every school has students who are academically disinterested, below grade level, and on their way toward dropping out of school. Rather than reserving video production solely for gifted and other high-achieving students, moviemaking often can be used to provide underachieving students another way to participate meaningfully in classroom work. At the same time that video production provides a possible academic entry for students with different learning styles, the process of planning and creating videos can lead to higher-level thinking and increased problem-solving ability for all students. Students with special needs and English language learners from kindergarten to high school also can participate. Students who might be considered "behavior problems" often can find leadership roles in the process of video production, and that allows these students to experience success and become productive members of a classroom environment.

In addition, video production allows teachers an opportunity to teach media literacy. In today's media-saturated society, it is essential for students to learn how to analyze and think critically about media messages. Although media literacy often is neglected due to time constraints and lack of teacher training, the discipline closely resembles traditional reading comprehension and can be taught through minilessons aligned with video production. By placing students inside short movie productions and asking them to make choices about the telling of their own stories, they will learn about media production from the inside out and begin to ask more intelligent questions about the commercial media that they consume.

GETTING STARTED

To get started, classrooms will need at least one working computer. Although older computers can be made to work, newer computers will include iMovie (in the case of Macintosh computers) or

Windows Movie Maker (in the case of a PC) and be ready for editing with little modification. Classrooms also need some way to capture images. Video cameras that use mini DV tapes are preferable for video editing, but other options include using digital still cameras (with video functions), Flip or other portable pocket video cameras, or even cell phones with video recording capability. Additional, optional equipment includes external microphones that improve audio quality and lighting that is reflected off walls and ceilings to avoid harsh shadows. Beginners tend to get hung up on buying the "right" equipment when, in actuality, the equipment makes little difference in the quality of the final production compared to adequate planning. It's also worth noting that the world has adjusted to a new "low-tech" aesthetic with the proliferation of online video-sharing sites and cell phone video cameras that capture and share low-quality video.

In classrooms that are just beginning to implement video production, it is reasonable to start with just one video project in the first year. If it is a teacher's first time making a movie, it also would not be advisable to begin the project in the first month of school when teachers are still establishing classroom procedures. Teachers, however, cannot wait until they have entirely mastered video production before getting started in their classrooms or they will never begin. Students often know more than their teachers about how to use cameras and video editing software. With a little practice, they can eclipse their teachers in terms of ability; even students as young as first grade can discover new ways of using software that teachers may have missed. Teachers who do not underestimate their students and are willing to learn alongside them can get started sooner and learn quickly on the job.

Teachers must model all parts of the moviemaking process, beginning with brainstorming filmable ideas and continuing with how to storyboard and write in script format. It is best for students to learn together by working in groups. When instructional time or resources are limited, teachers can begin by teaching just two or three students how to edit videos. Those students then can teach others and there is little to no time required for whole-group teaching.

STUDENT PRIVACY

Often schools are afraid to post student videos online due to privacy concerns. It probably is best not to post students' last names in conjunction with their online images. However, this means that educators *can* post student videos that may include their faces if they identify students only by first names (or by pseudonyms) and if they first have the students' and their parents' permission. Before posting any videos or photos of students online, teachers always should acquire parental permission and check with their individual school organizations to determine local policies and procedures. There often will be one or two students in a school whose parents will not allow them to be seen online, but this restriction should not entirely limit their ability to make movies. Students who are not allowed to be seen on camera still can participate in the writing, filming, editing, or other technical aspects of filmmaking.

COPYRIGHT

Video production likely will include music. Although fair use guidelines allow for teachers and students to use limited amounts of copyrighted materials for scholarly purposes, such as commenting on the copyrighted material for parody or journalism, the most common use of copyrighted material—using commercial music for movie soundtracks—is not allowed. Although there is little chance of teachers or students being sued for their use of copyrighted material, we cannot scold students for downloading music illegally if we do not respect music copyright in our own classrooms. Royalty-free music, or music that can be reused as long as credit to the author is given, is readily available on the Internet, such as on

"Royalty Free Music and Images" (http://tinyurl.com/24lm4qt) and "Flick School" (www.flickschool.com).

BASIC FILMMAKING

When it comes to creating a video, teachers need to help students think differently when working in a visual medium as compared to writing an essay. Amateurish videos use a lot of text titles to tell the story or rely too heavily on narration to move a story along. The classic mantra of filmmaking is literally to show, not tell. The question to be answered when making a movie is, "What do we want to *show* an audience to tell our story?" The visual nature of moviemaking applies to films of all genres, including both narratives and documentary videos. A Ken Burns documentary is no less visual than a mass-market blockbuster. If a student is turning an oral report into a video, then choices must be made about how to visually represent that report.

Just as writing follows a grammatical structure made up of words, sentences, and paragraphs, movie grammar is composed of shots and scenes. Unless filmed intentionally in one take, movies are generally made up of more than one shot. Students should make decisions about where to place the camera based on what is most important for audiences to see. This analysis ranks among the highest tiers of Bloom's taxonomy and leads to a greater understanding of commercially available media. In addition to focus, shot composition reveals information about psychology of characters and story subtext. For example, by placing the camera lower than the height of an actor, the actor can be made to look slightly menacing. By placing the camera higher than an actor and shooting down, the actor may seem smaller and less intimidating. Looking at short examples from commercial films takes little time but will greatly increase students' ability to plan their own projects and think critically about the choices involved in creating media. The goal of a video production program is not to create new Steven

Spielbergs (even if that might be an occasional by-product) but rather to foster critical thinking, teamwork, and problem-solving while increasing content knowledge and information retention.

CURRICULUM CONNECTIONS

The idea of integrating video production into the curriculum is not to create a new curriculum but instead to find ways of incorporating production projects into what teachers already are teaching. Short videos can take the place of oral reports and final papers or they can supplement those projects. Either way, teachers should understand that when done right making a video can be much more work than a final paper.

Although using any sort of video production in the classroom is almost sure to increase student engagement, the most successful projects focus on clear academic objectives. Assessment is a necessary component to measure the success of a particular video project. When focusing on reading fluency with a large group of English language learners, I used reader's theater combined with animated still pictures to tell the story of a first-grade horror film, *Tales from the Yard* (http://vimeo.com/4297297). In looking at student data, we saw that the number of students reading at benchmark increased by 20 percent in the months following the production as a result of rehearsing, producing, and reviewing the movie in connection with the reader's theater script.

When students create their own projects, the project itself can serve as the assessment tool. In *We See Animals Hiding*, students were taught to use the software but allowed to craft their own segments of the production. Although most students demonstrated their knowledge clearly, others needed reteaching based on their inability to clearly state how and why animals use camouflage as per the movie's objective (http://vimeo.com/4304508).

Some other clever examples of video projects in the field of language arts include sequels, prequels, adaptations, and genre studies. The genre of filmmaking itself can be taught as a discipline, as middle school teacher George Mayo shows on his class blog (http://lclprod.wordpress.com). History videos can re-create historical events, explain the causes of events, or reimagine what would have happened if historical decisions had been different as in the Minuteman movie by teacher Steven Katz (www.teachwith video.com/samples.html). In math and science, videos are a great medium to present nonlinguistic representations of abstract concepts and phenomena. In *Camouflage Jones* I attempted to use the film noir genre to tell a story of animal camouflage, a required unit in the Los Angeles Unified School District. Second-grade teacher Greg Paulsen uses clay animation and a classic rock cover tune to teach students about bats in *What I Like About Bats* (http://tinyurl .com/ilikebats).

POSTING VIDEOS ONLINE

There are several places to post videos online. Movies posted on YouTube have the potential to gain the biggest real-world audience. There are famous examples of students getting recording contracts or deals to direct lucrative television commercials as well as less famous examples of students getting their messages heard by politicians via the notice their movies received online. Unfortunately, YouTube tends to be blocked in many public school districts. Therefore, many teachers post movies in two places. First, they post on YouTube to gain audience and then they post on a site such as TeacherTube, SchoolTube, or Vimeo, depending on which works best and is not blocked in their own district. Each of these sites has different possible privacy settings. It is also possible to post videos to a school website but this requires additional technological know-how. The best of both worlds may be to post the movie to a commercial website and then use that site's embed code to make the movie accessible via the school website. Online video-hosting services typically are free, although some offer premium memberships with additional features and privacy settings. Remember to balance the potential for reaching an audience with student privacy.

SUMMARY

Video is not a language of the twenty-first century; it is a language of the twentieth century. Because of cost and equipment considerations, however, schools just now are starting to catch up. It is impossible to become an expert at creating videos by reading a single chapter or even a single book. At a certain point, teachers and schools must simply jump in whether or not they feel ready. By using available equipment and enlisting the help of students, teachers will get better with experience, and students will learn even if early projects don't go well. A school video-making culture begins to develop as soon as the first group of students has made its projects. Working with students to make movies brings school curricula to life.

Resources

American Film Institute Screen Education: www.afi.com/education/

Author's own site with examples of classroom movies and how-to links: www.videointheclassroom.com

Desler, G. (2010, July 23). *A case for filmmaking in the classroom.* BlogWalker. Retrieved from http://tinyurl.com/2cdaofx

Marco Torres's video production tips: www.flickschool.com

Royalty Free Music and Images List: http://tinyurl.com/24lm4qt

TLC using video editing for learning. (2007, January 5). Poway Unified home page. Retrieved from http://powayusd.sdcoe.k12.ca.us/projects/edtechcentral/digitalstorytelling/default.htm#Using_Video_Editing_in_the_Classroom

www.schooltube.com

www.teachertube.com

www.vimeo.com

www.youtube.com

CHAPTER 6

Virtual Schooling

Michael Barbour

and Richard E. Ferdig

Distance education at the K–12 level can take many forms. It ranges from the traditional print-based correspondence courses to instruction delivered through radio, television, satellite, or over the Internet (Clark, 2007). In this chapter, we focus on K–12 online learning generally and more specifically the virtual schools that offer instruction through online or blended formats.

The development of virtual schooling began in 1991 with a private school in California. However, it was the development of statewide initiatives that really drove the initial growth of K–12 virtual schools. In 1994 the State of Utah created the Utah e-School, which primarily focused on correspondence courses but also included some online offerings (Clark, 2003). This was followed by the Florida Virtual School and Virtual High School Global Consortium in 1996–97 (funded, respectively, through state and federal grants). These early initiatives were primarily designed to provide supplemental online learning opportunities for students located in brick-and-mortar schools. The first full-time virtual school began around 2000–01; full-time students currently account for the largest growth in virtual schooling (Watson, Gemin, Ryan, & Wicks, 2009).

This growth in virtual schools mirrored the growth in students taking online K–12 classes. It was estimated that forty thousand to fifty thousand K–12 students were taking online classes in the United States in 2001 (Clark, 2001). Less than a decade later, that number had grown to over one million, with many students enrolling in multiple courses (Picciano & Seaman, 2009). In their most recent *Keeping Pace with K–12 Online Learning* report, Watson, Gemin, Ryan, and Wicks (2009) described significant K–12 online learning activity in forty-five of the fifty states and the District of Columbia. Online learning at the K–12 level is growing exponentially; some predict that it will make up half of all K–12 education by 2020 (Christensen, Horn, & Johnson, 2008).

As the amount and popularity of virtual schooling has increased, there have been several other changes to ensure its continued growth. In 2006, Michigan became the first state to require that all students complete an online learning experience in order to graduate from high school. This has been followed by states such as New Mexico and Alabama, and several other jurisdictions currently are exploring the possibility. Other states, such as Georgia, Idaho, and Arizona, have introduced online teaching endorsements to their teacher certification process. Similarly, Michigan has revised its educational technology teaching standards. Three of the five standards are now directly related to K–12 online learning, which ensures that all teachers who gain this endorsement to their teaching certificate are prepared to design, deliver, and support virtual schooling.

Factors such as the growing number of K–12 students engaged in virtual schooling, legislation designed to encourage virtual schooling, and changes to teacher certification all point to an increased presence of virtual schooling in the K–12 system. In this chapter we review the different models and types of K–12 virtual schooling along with the changes in the role of the teacher caused by this new form of education. We also discuss what we know about virtual schooling based on the research that is currently available. Finally, we explore some of the issues that school administrators may wish to consider as they implement virtual schooling.

MODELS OF VIRTUAL SCHOOLING

Clark (2000) originally defined virtual schools as "a state approved and/or regionally accredited school that offers secondary credit courses through distance learning methods that include Internet-based delivery" (p. i). As virtual schooling has grown, the types of virtual school providers also have evolved. Today, virtual schools are often described or classified based on the following criteria:

- *Comprehensiveness*—supplemental program (individual courses) versus full-time school (full course load)
- *Reach*—district, multidistrict, state, multistate, national, global
- *Type*—district, magnet, contract, charter, private, home
- *Location*—school, home, other
- *Delivery*—asynchronous, synchronous, web, video-conferencing, and so on
- *Operational control*—local board, consortium, regional authority, university, state, independent, vendor
- *Type of instruction*—fully online, fully face-to-face, blending online and face-to-face
- *Grade level*—elementary, middle, high, and secondary
- *Teacher-student interaction*—high, moderate, low
- *Student-student interaction*—high, moderate, low (Watson, Gemin, Ryan, & Wicks, 2009) [Both of these last levels of interaction also can be "none" in the case of database-driven courses.]

The three most common classifications are *supplemental programs*, *full-time programs*, and *blended programs*. Supplement virtual schools are programs in which students are enrolled in a traditional physical school and enroll in one or more online courses to supplement their in-school courses. This is the model that describes most state-led programs (for example, Florida Virtual School, Innovative Digital Education and Learning New Mexico, ACCESS Alabama, or the Idaho Digital Learning Academy). However, full-time virtual schooling occurs when students are not enrolled in a brick-and-mortar school at all but complete all of their courses online. This is the model that describes many of the cyber charter schools (for example, Georgia Virtual Academy, Ohio Connections Academy, and Insight School of Colorado).

Blended learning occurs when students are enrolled in a brick-and-mortar school but their teachers make use of online resources as a part of their schooling. Similar to supplemental and full-time virtual schools, blended learning may take many formats. For example, VOISE Academy High School in Chicago is a blended program in which students attend a brick-and-mortar school but the course content is provided online; the teachers who are physically located in the building act as facilitators or learning coaches. Another example is in the State of Michigan, where many students enrolled in a brick-and-mortar school will complete a portion (often a unit) of one of their face-to-face courses online—with the course content and the primary instruction occurring in a course management system and the teacher again performing the role of facilitator.

MULTIPLE ROLES WITHIN VIRTUAL SCHOOLING

Within a virtual school, there are multiple roles and responsibilities that must be addressed (Davis, 2007).

Teacher

This role includes the presentation of activities, the management of pacing, interacting with students, assessing students, and interacting with parents and face-to-face site facilitators or mentors. According to Zucker (2005), the most common reasons given by school districts when asked why they use virtual schooling included the ability to offer courses that would not usually be offered at their school and the ability to offer Advanced Placement and other advanced-level courses. One of the reasons these courses are often unavailable is that there is no qualified teacher available to teach that course. For example, in her opening address at the 2008 Virtual School Symposium, Susan Patrick, the president of the International Association for K–12 Online Learning (iNACOL), stated there were 440 high schools in the State of Georgia but only eighty-eight qualified physics teachers. In these instances the virtual school teacher—or the teacher who is physically distant from the students and responsible for the instruction of that student—becomes an important role.

Designer

This role may or may not be undertaken by the teacher; the responsibilities include designing instructional materials and working in teams to construct online courses. Barbour (2005, 2007) described how teachers are primarily responsible for the design of virtual school courses at some virtual schools. Multimedia specialists might be used after the course has been designed to increase the interactive items in the course content. Alternative models have the teacher as a member of a larger team of web development specialists, project managers, and instructional designers (Johnston, 2004). And, finally, still other virtual schools require that virtual school instructors adapt the content as a part of their contract.

Facilitator

The facilitator has supervisory responsibility, mentoring face-to-face students taking online classes, acting as their advocate, proctoring exams, and assigning and recording grades along with being a soft skills coach. The virtual school site facilitator, often called the mentor or mediating teacher (m-teacher), is the role that is often neglected within the virtual school environment. This is the face-to-face, school-based teacher who has been assigned the role of loco parentis at the local level. Although the virtual school site facilitator is often the forgotten or overlooked teacher in the virtual school environment, it could be the most important of the three.

Other Roles

Depending on the nature of the virtual school program, there are other instructional roles that may be needed. Full-time programs, such as cyber charter schools, also use a learning coach as a part of their instructional support team (Connections Academy, 2004). As most full-time online students do not attend a traditional brick-and-mortar school, there is no virtual school facilitator at the local level to help support the student. Many full-time virtual schools enlist the support of a learning coach to perform this role, and as most students complete their online studies at home the learning coach is often a parent, guardian, or other relative. Depending on the specific full-time program, the actual instructional role of the learning coach varies. In some programs, the learning coach is simply responsible for supervising the student—particularly during assessments—and providing that sense of local encouragement. However, in other instances the learning coach is the primary source of instruction and content-based support.

RESEARCH ON K–12 VIRTUAL SCHOOLING

Due to the relative young age of K–12 virtual schooling, the field still lacks a strong research base on its effectiveness and associated best practices. However, there are at least five important research findings from the work that has been completed to date.

Virtual Schooling Works

Perhaps the most important research finding is that K–12 virtual schooling works. In 2004, a meta-analysis was completed that found only fourteen studies related to K–12 online learning. However, those fourteen studies provided evidence that K–12 students learned as much as or more online than they did in their face-to-face environments (Cavanaugh, Gillan, Kromrey, Hess, & Blomeyer, 2004). In 2009, a similar meta-analysis was completed by the U.S. Department of Education. The study found that, "on average, online learning students performed better than those receiving face-to-face instruction" (Means, Toyama, Murphy, Bakia, & Jones, 2009, p. ix).

Although these are positive findings for the K–12 community, there have been some questions about the selection nature of students in the virtual school samples in these studies—that is, that students are self-selecting into virtual learning and thus may not be representative of students as a whole (Barbour, 2009). Additionally, this research does not suggest that simply putting content online works, and more research is required to determine best practices in virtual teaching and learning in K–12 environments.

Teachers Need More Training

Unfortunately, less than 40 percent of all virtual school teachers in the United States reported receiving professional development before they began teaching online (Rice & Dawley, 2007) and even fewer indicate that they receive any preparation in their university-based teacher-training programs (Project Tomorrow and Blackboard, 2010). Many K–12 teacher education programs have yet to embrace K–12 online learning; as such, many preservice and in-service teachers are unprepared to teach online. Simply because they have teaching experience does not mean that teachers will succeed online. DiPietro, Ferdig, Black, and Preston (2008) found that there were skills that were unique to the online teacher— skills that could not simply be ported from face-to-face instruction.

Virtual Schooling Can Work for At-Risk Students

Part of the allure of virtual K–12 education is its promise of reaching stay-at-home teen moms, expelled and detained students, students who need remediation, and other at-risk students. A recent study examined twenty-seven students who had dropped out of school but returned to finish their coursework in an online environment (Ferdig, 2010). Data revealed that all twenty-seven students did as well as, if not better than, their face-to-face counterparts enrolled in the same classes. All twenty-seven students passed at least one of their classes and each was on his or her way back to high school graduation. This study provided evidence that students *could succeed*; however, when organizers replicated the struggles that students had in face-to-face settings (for example, lectures without support structures), students replicated their face-to-face failures.

Online Students Need Support

In their evaluation of the ACCESS Alabama online program, Roblyer, Freeman, Stabler, and Schneidmiller (2007) found that "facilitators who are directly working with students day-by-day are key to the success of the program" (p. 11). Other studies have found the same outcomes (for example, Ferdig & Black, 2008). Students always need scaffolding and support; it is a key component of most pedagogical strategies. However, when they go online and lose direct contact with a face-to-face instructor, they often need the mentoring role of another teacher, a school counselor, a facilitator, or a parent. These support personnel provide motivation, technical support, and even logistical solutions for students (for example, enrollment).

Data Is Critical

Data-driven decision making is important to improving teaching and learning. Online environments provide easier access to recorded data; however, that does not mean that the data will be collected, analyzed, or shared with students, parents, teachers, and school leaders. The Virtual School Clearinghouse (www.vsclearinghouse.com) was built in 2006 with a grant from the BellSouth Foundation, later the AT&T Foundation (Ferdig, 2006). The goal of the grant was to help schools collect and analyze data. The research team initially found that both face-to-face and virtual schools were not collecting as much data as necessary to be able to ask and answer important education questions. Additionally, if they were collecting data, they only were collecting data about the teacher and the students. In online learning environments, there also are data that are available about the course (for example, who built it), the course instance (for example, when it was taught and by whom), the school or entity from which the student enrolled, and who is involved with the student's instruction (for example, parent, mentor, facilitator, and so on). Each of these components is key to making effective data-driven instructional decisions and to informing the research in this young field.

SUGGESTED OUTCOMES
FOR SCHOOL LEADERS

K–12 online learning is increasing exponentially as is the number of students enrolling. School leaders, either by their choices or the choices of teachers and students under their care, can embrace virtual schooling in a number of different ways. On one end is the supervision of students taking courses online while in their school; on the opposite end is the creation of blended and online environments. In either case, there are several key outcomes and concerns for school leaders:

1. *Train your teachers.* Teachers in face-to-face schools may never become online or blended instructors. However, at the very least, they probably will have students in their classes who take online courses. Teachers need to have a good understanding of K–12 online learning and the support they might have to provide for their students. A school leader who supports an online or blended teaching environment should never assume that face-to-face instructors can teach online simply because they have years of teaching experience.

2. *Provide support for students.* Students taking online classes need administrative support (for example, enrolling in classes), technological support (for example, access to a computer lab), and, in some cases, content help. Brick-and-mortar schools usually assign one person to do all of these things, generally the school counselor. Forward-thinking school leaders find ways to create mentors or mentoring teams for students taking online and blended content so that they have a better chance to succeed.

3. *Lead by example.* School leaders wishing to create online and blended programs should understand that many teachers have never taken an online class. Asking them to teach online or in blended environments without first having the experience of learning in them is like putting the cart before the horse. School leaders should consider finding ways to offer online and blended professional development so that teachers can learn in the environment in which they will teach.

4. *Collect, analyze, and use data.* Data are important for leaders. Therefore, a simple recommendation is to help leaders find ways to analyze existing best practices through data collection. A more challenging suggestion is to find ways and then share those analyses with the shareholders. Find ways to assess students beyond just once or twice a year, then find ways to share those outcomes with teachers, mentors, and parents throughout the year. Online learning presents a wealth of new information that is collected daily; simply having the data available does not mean they will instantly be ready for public consumption. The Virtual School Clearinghouse has existing templates that can be downloaded and analyzed for free.

5. *Join the community.* There is an existing community of leaders who have participated in discussions about pedagogy, technology, and practice in K–12 online learning. Find ways to connect to those communities. The International Association for K–12 Online Learning (iNACOL; www.inacol .org) hosts an annual conference and has online forums and articles for support and guidance.

SUMMARY

In sum, online education is a rapidly growing medium for teaching and learning at the K–12 level. Early research indicates that K–12 virtual schooling has promise for multiple audiences. However, simply building online content and hoping for success will not work. School leaders should be optimistic about the potential but thoughtful when it comes to implementation.

References

Barbour, M. K. (2005). *Evaluation of the Illinois Virtual High School course development process.* Aurora: Illinois Virtual

High School. Retrieved from www.imsa.edu/programs/ivhs/pdfs/course_development_eval_2005–10.pdf

Barbour, M. K. (2007). Principles of effective web-based content for secondary school students: Teacher and developer perceptions. *Journal of Distance Education, 21*(3), 93–114. Retrieved from www.jofde.ca/index.php/jde/article/view/30

Barbour, M. K. (2009). Today's student and virtual schooling: The reality, the challenges, the promise. *Journal of Distance Learning, 13*(1), 5–25.

Cavanaugh, C., Gillan, K. J., Kromrey, J., Hess, M., & Blomeyer, R. (2004). *The effects of distance education on K–12 student outcomes: A meta-analysis.* Naperville, IL: Learning Point Associates.

Christensen, C. M., Horn, M. B., & Johnson, C. W. (2008). *Disrupting class: How disruptive innovation will change the way the world learns.* New York: McGraw-Hill.

Clark, T. (2000). *Virtual high schools: State of the states—a study of virtual high school planning and preparation in the United States.* Center for the Application of Information Technologies, Western Illinois University. Retrieved from www.imsa.edu/programs/ivhs/pdfs/stateofstates.pdf

Clark, T. (2001). *Virtual schools: Trends and issues—a study of virtual schools in the United States.* San Francisco: Western Regional Educational Laboratories. Retrieved from www.wested.org/online_pubs/virtualschools.pdf

Clark, T. (2003). Virtual and distance education in American schools. In M. G. Moore & W. G. Anderson (Eds.), *Handbook of distance education* (pp. 673–699). Mahwah, NJ: Lawrence Erlbaum.

Clark, T. (2007). Virtual and distance education in North American schools. In M. G. Moore (Ed.), *Handbook of Distance Education* (2nd ed.) (pp. 473–490). Mahwah, NJ: Lawrence Erlbaum.

Connections Academy. (2004). *Learning without boundaries: How to make virtual schooling work for you.* Baltimore: Author.

Davis, N. E. (2007, November). *Teacher education for virtual schools.* A presentation at the annual Virtual School Symposium, Louisville, KY. Retrieved from http://ctlt.iastate.edu/~tegivs/TEGIVS/publications/VS%20Symposium2007.pdf

DiPietro, M., Ferdig, R. E., Black, E. W., & Preston, M. (2008). Best practices in teaching K–12 online: Lessons learned from Michigan Virtual School teachers. *Journal of Interactive Online Learning, 7*(1). Retrieved from www.ncolr.org/jiol/issues/getfile.cfm?volID=7&IssueID=22&ArticleID=113

Ferdig, R. E. (2006). Principal investigator for funded grant proposal ($600,000) entitled *Establishing a framework to strengthen virtual high schools: A collaborative initiative to improve student performance and quality of instruction.* Atlanta, GA: BellSouth Foundation.

Ferdig, R. E. (2010). *Understanding the role and applicability of K–12 online learning to support student dropout recovery efforts.* Report presented to Michigan Virtual School, East Lansing, Michigan.

Ferdig, R. E., & Black, E. W. (2008, December). *Surprises in online learning: What the data show.* Paper presented at the Michigan Virtual School Symposium, East Lansing, Michigan.

Johnston, S. (2004). Teaching any time, any place, any pace. In C. Cavanaugh (Ed.), *Development and management of virtual schools: Issues and trends* (pp. 116–134). Hershey, PA: Idea Group.

Means, B., Toyama, Y., Murphy, R., Bakia, M., & Jones, K. (2009). *Evaluation of evidence-based practices in online learning: A meta-analysis and review of online learning studies.* Washington, DC: U.S. Department of Education, Office of Planning, Evaluation, and Policy Development.

Picciano, A. G., & Seaman, J. (2009). *K–12 online learning: A 2008 follow-up of the survey of U.S. school district administrators.* Needham, MA: Alfred P. Sloan Foundation. Retrieved from www.sloanconsortium.org/publications/survey/pdf/k-12_online_learning_2008.pdf

Project Tomorrow and Blackboard. (2010). *Learning in the 21st century: 2010 trends update.* Irvine, CA: Authors. Retrieved from www.blackboard.com/Solutions-by-Market/K-12/Learn-for-K12/Leadership-Views/Education-in-the-21st-Century.aspx

Rice, K., & Dawley, L. (2007). *Going virtual! The status of professional development for K–12 online teachers.* Boise, ID: Boise State University. Retrieved from http://edtech.boisestate.edu/going virtual/goingvirtual1.pdf

Roblyer, M. D., Freeman, J., Stabler, M., & Schneidmiller, J. (2007). *External evaluation of the Alabama ACCESS initiative: Phase 3 report.* Eugene, OR: International Society for Technology in Education. Retrieved from http://accessdl.state.al.us/2006Evaluation.pdf

Watson, J. F., Gemin, B., Ryan, J., & Wicks, M. (2009). *Keeping pace with K–12 online learning: A review of state-level policy and practice.* Naperville, IL: Learning Point Associates. Retrieved from www.kpk12.com/downloads/KeepingPace09-fullreport.pdf

Zucker, A. (2005). *A study of student interaction and collaboration in the virtual high school.* Naperville, IL: Learning Point Associates.

Social Media Is Changing the Way We Live and Learn

Sheryl Nussbaum-Beach

On Wednesday, January 13, 2010, as Haiti was dealing with the aftermath of a catastrophic 7.0 magnitude earthquake that later was reported to have killed two hundred thousand people (Pew Research Center, 2010), the shockwaves spread around the world through social media. Through the immediacy of Twitter, we received firsthand accounts of the devastation by a few dozen people on the ground in Haiti whose Twitter streams became live news feeds (Epatko, 2010). This put Twitter users on a level playing field with the mainstream media outlets they once depended on for breaking news. During the first forty-eight hours following the disaster, 2.3 million tweets including the words *Haiti* or *Red Cross* were shared globally. Thousands of those tweets also included *90999*, the number that could be texted to make a $10 donation to the Red Cross relief effort. From behind laptops and clenched cell phones, concerned citizens were connecting not only to share and learn but to become involved and make a difference. On Facebook, the group "Earthquake Haiti" was created and had nearly 170,000 members by the following day. By the end of the week, social media had helped raise $8 million for the Red Cross relief effort, more than has ever been generated in a similar campaign (Pew Research Center, 2010).

This social movement was unprecedented because the massive, tightly woven networks that enabled it were like none we had seen before. We've entered a world where it is easy to form groups around our interests. It's a world where we can participate and drive a social movement for greater good from anywhere, at any time, with devices with which we are so comfortable that we take them for granted.

Social media has offered us a platform where we can learn from and with the smartest people we "meet" from around the world, whenever we need to or are ready to. That goes for even young children, such as philanthropist Laura Stockman of the blog *25 Days to Make a Difference*, who not only can change the world but also can change their own learning worlds in the process (Stockman, 2008). And it goes for professional learning in communities where participatory technologies allow us to connect quickly and easily to receive "just-in-time answers" and support, the kind of support that changes us for the better. The social media tools themselves have not changed us as a society but the way we use them certainly has made its impact.

It seems we are living out our lives in an era of dueling tensions: both physical and virtual spaces compete for our attention. Through an endless choice of social tools we perform a balancing act of seemingly competitive actions vying for the forefront: private versus public, trusting versus cautious, sharing versus withholding, collaborative versus individualistic, and more. Our behavior online represents a paradigm shift in the fundamental way we find ourselves as participants in society. We are connected and therefore we are empowered to be part of the global conversation that can change the world. Communities and networks are the infrastructure through which we converse.

This moment presents us with difficult challenges and huge opportunities. The opportunities go far beyond the simple ability to publish to the web, far beyond the simple use of cool apps on our smart phones. They revolve around connecting, forming groups, and creating self-organized, personal classrooms in which we can learn and do good work together and create change in very nontraditional ways.

To take advantage of these opportunities, we first have to be willing to share our ideas openly and honestly. Trust is what makes risk-taking possible. In fact, trust is a huge piece of the shift we are seeing as a result of social media. However, although trust is needed to become participants in a culture of content producers, the trend is actually shifting in the other direction, at least in how we are sharing content as consumers.

Through the use of social media, advertisers have been able to share authentic, credible stories about their products. Yet, according to Edelman's latest trust barometer, the percentage of those who saw their friends and colleagues as credible sources has dropped by almost half—from 45 percent to 25 percent—since 2008 (Bush, 2010). Some blame the rampant "friending" that takes place on social networking sites as having diluted the value of peer-to-peer networks with disingenuous marketing efforts and popularity contests. We place more trust in those we know personally than those we have met or listened to online, making building trust through transparency and openness now more important than ever.

This openness and transparency through social media has completely shaken our expectations of privacy. The real world affords us many ways of keeping public and private information separate, while the online world's instant, global, and permanent footprint blurs that distinction (Shirky, 2008). Those of us unaccustomed to the manners and norms of this connected world struggle with concerns about what to share and what not to share. Our discomfort about sharing private information makes us question our full participation in online spaces. At the same time, when we share we experience the rewards of joining a connected network of learners who join in what some are calling a global brain (Heylighen, 2008).

In contrast, the generation of children growing up today does not possess the same expectations of privacy that make many adults uncomfortable with social media. Today's children are growing up in a new culture of privacy, where they go about their lives aware that they have an audience. In this culture, it's comfortable to be open, honest, and share with transparency (Nussbaum, 2007).

What we gain from giving up some of our privacy and offering transparency is access to a global or planetary brain. According to Heylighen (2008), this global brain is an "emerging, collectively intelligent network that is formed by the people of this planet together with the computers, knowledge bases, and communication links that connect them together" (p. 305). Access to this instantly connected global community of networked learners changes our perceptions and expectations of the world around us.

With the ability to virtually meet up with people from all over the world with the click of a few buttons, we can collaborate in ways that just weren't possible at the turn of the century. This ability to collaborate shifts our locally centric way of life to one with a more global perspective. We think less about our individual lives and more about society, and we have more consideration for the world around us. Recently, I was asked to present for Microsoft's Innovative Schools program in a virtual university session held online. I was in awe as, one by one, schools in countries from around the world logged on and, in their very rich accents, introduced themselves and gave their definition of what it meant to be a global citizen in today's connected world. I remember thinking how different the perspectives were from mine and how I would be a better person for having heard them.

If social media is changing us, then how do we gain the most from our participation in this planetary brain? Shirky (2008) suggests that there are four stages to mastering the connected world: sharing, cooperating, collaboration, and collective action. Let's look at each of these as it relates to our roles as instructional leaders.

Sharing is the key to connecting online and it's a fundamental skill of network literacy. Social media provides us the tools to make sharing easy. But we need to understand sharing within the context of what happens after we share. We share because we want to connect with others around our passions, not simply to communicate. Sharing makes us become "clickable," findable by others. If I can't find you, I can't learn from you. Sharing leads to connecting, which is the starting place for network-building and cooperating.

Cooperating in networks is typically done through the sharing of ideas and resources but without much accountability, action, or follow-through on the ideas. As you share and connect with other educational leaders, you begin to build a collective identity and effi-cacy. Cooperation in online spaces is really about connections and relationship-building. It is from those relationships that opportunities develop to collaborate and form communities.

Collaboration requires the best efforts of those involved to build something together. An intimacy beyond a networking relation-ship develops as each learner contributes his or her own gifts and ideas to improve and grow the planetary brain. Collaboration within a community can lead to outcomes that affect society for the greater good and can result in projects or efforts that display the wisdom of the crowd at its best. Collaboration within a school means that we should approach goals as connected learners who are depen-dent on the gifting, skills, knowledge, and talents of each other as a means for meeting the needs of today's students. The simple truth is that there is a limit to how much we can learn if we function in the silos of traditional school leadership.

Collective action in a community often results in positive global change. Social media offer us tools to connect in ways that will change society for the better. This is especially true in educa-tion as students and teachers become colearners in the creation of projects that not only align with curricular goals but also create an awareness of social justice issues and how to solve them from a global perspective. Educators, operating as activists or change agents, can collaboratively research an issue and act collectively toward solving it. Social media tools provide the reach to our voices and the amplification to our efforts in viral ways that move beyond anything we have done as individuals in the past. It is the wise educational leader who understands this and creates an open leadership plan that incorporates collective action as a goal.

Social media is breaking down barriers that make cultures unique. It's blending us and we're becoming more alike because we are sharing ideas. This kind of connectedness can have profound effects as it helps us settle issues of global conflict and suffering. Shift the setting to the school house and think of the legacy we could leave if we enabled our students to share, connect, and collaborate with others. What would be the result if we helped them build relationships and networks with an understanding of the power a voice and a platform could make?

Social media has changed the way that we connect with people around us and, in essence, who we are and what we will become. Our children are growing up in a world where they can launch a social movement from their laptops (Gladwell, 2009). As educational leaders, we can transform our schools into places that truly meet the needs of today's learners. But first we must be willing to understand and own the tools and shifts ourselves: you cannot give away what you do not own. It will be through the modeling and support of ongoing professional development designed to leverage teacher-selected connections and community that collective action, not just crowd sourcing (outsourcing work to a group), will become a venue through which school leaders can make the world a better place.

References

Bush, M. (2010, February 8). In age of friending, consumers trust their friends less. *Advertising Age*. Retrieved from http://adage.com/article?article_id=141972

Epatko, L. (2010, February 16). Haiti quake propels use of twitter as disaster-relief tool. *PBS News Hour*. Retrieved from www.pbs.org/newshour/rundown/2010/02/haiti-quake-propels-twitter-community-mapping-efforts.html

Gladwell, M. (2009, May 12). *10 ways to change the world through social media*. Retrieved from http://mashable.com/2009/05/12/social-media-change-the-world

Heylighen, F. (2008). The emergence of a global brain. In M. Tovey (Ed.), *Collective intelligence: Creating a prosperous world at peace*. Oakton, VA: Earth Intelligence Network.

Nussbaum, E. (2007, February 12). Say everything. *New York Magazine*. Retrieved from http://nymag.com/news/features/27341/index2.html

Pew Research Center. (2010, January 21). *Social media provide first-hand accounts, direct action on Haiti*. Retrieved from http://pewresearch.org/pubs/1471/social-media-haiti-earthquake-major-role-fundraising

Shirky, C. (2008). *Here comes everybody: The power of organizing without organizations*. New York: Penguin Press.

Stockman, L. (2008). *25 days to make a difference*. Retrieved from http://twentyfivedays.wordpress.com

CHAPTER 7

One-to-One Computing

Chris Lehmann

and Pamela Livingston

Few, if any, schoolwide improvement programs have the depth and breadth of one-to-one (1:1) computing. One-to-one programs—a digital assistant, preferably a laptop or tablet, in every student's hand—are the holy grail of educational technology infusion. Leaders moving in this direction or shoring up existing 1:1 will find a holistic approach works best. But how a school implements its 1:1 initiative will determine its success or failure.

A digital device in every student's hand requires a collaborative vision of what the school can now accomplish, including the following:

- A powerful change in pedagogy
- A shift toward student centricity
- A well-defined set of goals
- A plan for professional development around achieving pedagogical and technological goals

- A strategy for technology support
- Attention to logistical issues that arise
- A way to regularly assess the program
- Commitment toward a sustainable future

At its most basic, a 1:1 computing program gives students the opportunity to interact with their educational world in a way that most closely mirrors the rest of the society. How many adults would be willing to share their work computer with four or five other people? And yet, in most schools, that is what we ask students to do. With a digital device in every student's hand, schools can find themselves unshackled from the limits of space and schedule, allowing students to learn, create, and communicate in powerful ways.

Schools wanting more than the basics will find that 1:1 education is a disruptive technology—one that challenges the norm of traditional schooling. Leaders of 1:1 recognize that stakeholders need be involved in building a new vision for education in their community. Administrators, teachers, students, and parents might have very different ideas about how the technology will alter the landscape of the school. Teachers may be nervous about how the technology will change their practice. Parents may have concerns about inappropriate use of technology by students. And, without a doubt, administrators can and should have dozens of questions about how this will change every aspect of school.

All stakeholders should be encouraged to dream big about the changes that 1:1 can offer. Of equal importance is the question, "What is the worst consequence of our best ideas?" One-to-one computing is not a panacea. If a community does not engage in deep reflection on the potential changes to the educational landscape, there is the chance that they will become reactionary when, inevitably, something goes wrong. Having all stakeholders as part of the planning process means the likelihood of powerful, meaningful change is great.

One way to think about the pedagogical change is that a 1:1 program should allow schools to make technology ubiquitous, necessary, and invisible. In a 1:1 environment, students have the technology with them at all times. It does not require a special trip to a lab or signing out a cart. This means that students can have constant access to the world around them. Resources for creating, synthesizing, researching, writing, presenting, and publishing are solidly in the hands of the learner, not distributed by the teacher. Teachers have to learn how to work this potential into their planning and classroom management. Students have to learn how to manage the productivity potential of the device as well as the distractibility potential. Used purposefully, 1:1 creates classrooms where teachers are facilitators and mentors, guiding students through learning and creation in powerful ways. In this model, students can be empowered creators and synthesizers of learning artifacts; build web pages, podcasts, and films; and connect their ideas with the world around them. When all embrace their new roles, it stops being about the technology and becomes about the work. When students and teachers stop talking about their laptops and instead use them in an authentic way toward common educational goals, a shared learning vision has been achieved.

With that common vision comes the necessary examination of what needs to change. The most obvious questions center on curriculum. Here are some of the questions that administrators should consider when moving into a 1:1 environment:

- What are the resources necessary to support the new teaching and learning paradigm?
- What will learning spaces populated by digital assistants look like?
- How will a shared learning community and schoolwide communication now be enhanced?

- How will you take advantage of the home-to-school possibilities?

- How will you support the hardware, network, and software and ensure that continual availability is the norm?

- How will you solve logistical issues including transportation, battery life, damage, and electricity?

- How will your teachers plan in this model to best harness the use of the tools for the students?

- How will your school use "traditional" information sources such as textbooks? Will they become classroom resources? Will students still need to take them home?

- How will assessment change in this model?

The classroom empowered with 1:1 changes as well. In a traditional classroom, students often come to class to receive information from a teacher. But in a 1:1 laptop environment, students obtain information in myriad ways. The challenge then becomes to reimagine the classroom to make it the place where students and teachers come together face-to-face to create shared knowledge. Many of the traditional pathways of our classrooms reflect the vision of a world of information scarcity but a 1:1 laptop program transforms school from a model of information scarcity to one of information abundance. Other questions will then follow:

- How will teachers manage their classes differently to harness the tools?

- What structures of the classroom become obsolete in this new paradigm?

- What work is best suited for online work? What work remains best completed offline or face-to-face?

- How will students and teachers take advantage of a networked world to ensure that their classrooms become windows to the world, not isolated cells?

It is important not to underestimate the changes to the lives of teachers in this new model. From curriculum design to classroom management to role of teacher and learner to record-keeping, every aspect of the teaching life is different with 1:1 computing. There is much relearning that has to happen to fully realize the potential of the technology, with professional development being of paramount importance. Learning must be focused on more than just the how-to of computing. Teachers will find they need to investigate how their teaching will change:

- How should teaching and learning change to reflect the new shared vision of school?

- What assumptions and behaviors will teachers release in terms of their instructional roles in order to achieve a more student-centered model?

- What are the new structures of teaching that should be implemented to achieve the vision?

- How will teachers collaborate to enable innovation to spread from class to class?

- What are the essential technological tools that all teachers should know how to use?

- What are the curricular tools (unit planning devices, rubrics for grading, and so on) that can help teachers reach their goals?

- How will teachers assess the new artifacts of learning that students can create?

- How can the teachers use the 1:1 laptop experience as a way to create a shared language of teaching and learning across the entire school?

Another challenge that schools face in a 1:1 environment is technological support. The invisibility of technology in a 1:1 environment goes away quickly if students and teachers cannot use the technology in a whenever and wherever fashion. In industry, suggested user-to-tech support ratios often are around 100:1 (http://news.zdnet.com/html/z/wb/6099383.html), or one full-time technical support specialist per one hundred computer users. Schools rarely have the budgets to match that ratio, but the success or failure of a 1:1 program often can hinge on whether or not the technology works. Given what is almost always a less-than-ideal technical support budget, schools do have an important resource that can both enhance the tech-support options and become a powerful pedagogical tool—students. Programs such as Generation YES (http://genyes.org) and MOUSE (www.mouse.org) can help schools create student tech teams that empower participants to become part of the solution for their schools. Schools such as the Denver School of Science and Technology, the Urban School of San Francisco, and many districts in Maine also have successfully used students for technical support and even for professional development.

However, technical support goes beyond considering "who fixes the machines." A technical support plan also should consider what the online resources and systems are for schools, who manages them, how new services are rolled out, and how decisions get made about all technical services. A list of potential questions for administrators to ask includes the following:

- Given your vision for 1:1 at your school, what devices best meet your needs? Laptops? Netbooks? Tablets? iPads? Mobile phones?

- What is the pathway for repairs? What can you do in-house? What needs to be part of a service contract?

- What backup batteries, chargers, laptops, and other devices will be available and how will they be signed out and managed?

- Will you provide insurance to cover damaged or stolen equipment and who will pay for this—the school or parents?

- What role can students play in supporting a 1:1 rollout?

- How will you handle lost, stolen, or broken-beyond-repair laptops?

- What is the necessary technological infrastructure to maintain an effective program?

- What online tools (course management systems, student information systems, schoolwide e-mail, content management systems, and so on) are needed, who will have access, and how will they be managed?

- How will the technology support staff work with the instructional team to ensure that student learning is always driving the decisions made?

- How will you ensure there is enough electrical power, wireless access points, and a robust-enough network to support roaming digital devices?

Despite all of this careful planning, the pace of change still can be powerfully frustrating. You won't achieve all your goals in your first year. Or your second. And by the time you get to your third, you will have learned lessons that should make you change some of your original goals. By your fourth year you may need a complete revisit of your goals and refresh your direction. Setting smart, achievable goals that can be revisited over time is an important part of success. The evolutionary process should include pedagogical goals, infrastructure goals, budgetary goals, and school structure goals.

Perhaps the most challenging part about 1:1 computing is that, despite twenty years of 1:1 schools all over the world, we are just at the very early days of this movement. Whatever solutions your school comes to today will evolve as technology continues to evolve. We are learning more every day about what it means to be in a networked world, and how we create schools that reflect our changing world is an ever-evolving process. The only thing you can be certain of is more change.

SUMMARY

This chapter is, in many respects, an attempt to codify a series of questions that 1:1 schools have had to answer, whether they did so deliberately or on the fly. It is meant to prepare you for the many issues that you will face on the way to a successful 1:1 program. What it does not do is speak to the influential, authentic change you will see if your school does this well. When combined with a powerful change in pedagogical practice, a 1:1 computing program can help students and teachers create a learning environment that is truly transformative for all involved. The potential to create new ideas and solve problems when a digital device is in the hands of your students—along with access to the open-ended, accessible tools of Web 2.0—can move schools from enclosed institutions surrounded by four walls to organizations at the forefront of deep and expansive learning.

CHAPTER 8

Free and Open Source Software

Tom Hoffman

Peer under the hood of the various innovative technologies and social media platforms discussed in the rest of this book and you will find one common thread: they almost all incorporate free and open source software in a significant way.

In some cases, important applications are completely open source: Wikipedia's Wikimedia server, WordPress's blogging engine (http://wordpress.org), and the Moodle learning management system (http://moodle.org), for example. Innumerable others are built primarily from open source databases, programming languages, web servers, operating systems, and other key components. Examples include Twitter, Facebook, blogs, wikis, podcast servers, photo-sharing sites such as Flickr, and other social media tools. According to Gartner research vice president Mark Driver (Brodkin, 2007), at least 80 percent of all commercial software will contain significant amounts of open source code: "Open source is going to come into your network whether you like it or not," Driver said. "It has become completely impractical to avoid the subject at all."

Increasingly, the technologies we use to access these services also are open source. The open source WebKit-rendering engine is used to display web pages and other user interface elements in Apple's Safari, Google Chrome, and Adobe's Creative Suite. WebKit powers browsers on iPhone, Android, BlackBerry, Accenture's Symbian, and Palm webOS phones. The open source Linux kernel is the foundation of operating systems running everything from IBM mainframes to Android phones, from Ubuntu netbooks to airline seatback entertainment systems. If you're not Amish, you probably already are a daily user of open source software, either directly or indirectly.

Free and open source software has been around a long time. It is integral to the pace of innovation and growth in the Internet economy and its influence and importance continues to grow. Open source is not a trend or a fad or an idealistic flight of fancy; it is not going away and it should be part of a school's or district's long-term technology strategy.

WHAT IS FREE AND OPEN SOURCE SOFTWARE?

The terms *free software* and *open source software* represent different ways to look at the same phenomenon. Functionally, both perspectives share a consistent core definition as described in this case by the free software definition:

> Free software is a matter of the users' freedom to run, copy, distribute, study, change and improve the software. More precisely, it means that the program's users have the four essential freedoms, as described in the Free Software Definition:
>
> - The freedom to run the program, for any purpose (freedom 0).
> - The freedom to study how the program works, and change it to make it do what you wish (freedom 1).

- The freedom to redistribute copies so you can help your neighbor (freedom 2).

- The freedom to distribute copies of your modified versions to others (freedom 3). By doing this you can give the whole community a chance to benefit from your changes. (GNU Operating System, 2011)

Software distributed under licenses that meet these conditions is free software; software that does not meet those terms is not. The open source definition is longer and contains different emphasis, but in practice it is not significantly different (Open Source Initiative, 2011).

To rephrase the previous definition in a way more directly relevant to educators, free and open source software allows schools to do the following:

- Use the software at as many sites or seats as the school would like at no licensing cost.

- Modify or customize the software or pay someone else to do so to suit the school's needs.

- Give students and teachers copies of the software so they have full access both at home and in the future.

- Collaborate with other schools, businesses, and other entities to promote, distribute, and receive improvements to the software.

FREE SOFTWARE: LIBRE OR GRATIS?

The *free* in *free software* does not refer to cost but rather to the user's freedom. In Spanish, the term used is *libre* (freedom), not *gratis* (without charge). Free and open source software is not anticommercial or anticapitalist. With open source software, you do not pay to obtain a license to use the software. You can and in many cases should expect to pay for services related to the software, such as support, training, documentation, customization, installation and set-up, or distribution—just as you also do for proprietary software.

THINGS THAT ARE NOT FREE OR OPEN SOURCE SOFTWARE

Sometimes software is made available under licenses that appear to be free or open source but are not. The following sections explain the differences.

Made with Open Source

In many cases, particularly in the web applications mentioned at the beginning of the chapter such as Flickr or Facebook, software is written with and includes open source components but the end product is not available to the user under an open source license.

Free to Use

Just because one can use an application at no cost, whether on the web or installed on your computer, does not mean the application fits the long-established definition of *free software*. Free and open source software also gives you the right to study, modify, and redistribute the work indefinitely.

Noncommercial Licensed Software

Schools often use software at no cost under a noncommercial license; that is, a school can use it for free but a business must pay to use or sell it. This software is explicitly not open source because it violates "the freedom to run the program for any purpose."

Open Standards

Open standards define standard file types and formats to allow applications to exchange data. They are good things insofar as they help systems work together and prevent customers from becoming locked into one vendor. Open standards often go hand-in-hand with open source software but are not a replacement, in part because the real-world implementation of complex standards often falls short of the ideal.

WHAT ARE SCHOOLS DOING WITH FREE AND OPEN SOURCE SOFTWARE?

Schools are using free and open source software in a number of interesting and powerful ways. Some are profiled in the following.

High Profile: 1:1

The open source deployments making the biggest splash have been 1:1 computing initiatives. Paying $50, $100, or more for software licenses per seat was not so painful when computers cost over $1,000 and were purchased by the dozens. Now that netbook and desktop hardware prices are under $300 and falling—and schools are purchasing these lower-cost computers by the hundreds and thousands—software costs must come down proportionally.

Starting in 2004, the Indiana Office of Learning Technologies' inACCESS (www.doe.in.gov/olt/InACCESS/) program successfully put PCs on the desks of about half of the high school English classrooms statewide in an effort to boost writing achievement, reaching over 150,000 students. Using Linux and other open source applications, they kept the software costs under $5 per seat and the total hardware and software cost under $300 per seat.

Saugus Union School District in California, led by director of information services and technology Jim Klein, has deployed 2,400 sub-$500 netbooks to students, all of which run a version of Ubuntu Linux (http://ubuntu.com) customized by district staff. In keeping with the open source process, Saugus has made its customized operating system available to other schools at no cost, saving other schools around the country even more administrative expenses (Saugus Union School District, 2011).

Many other 1:1 computing initiatives enhance their Windows or Mac OS images with a variety of open source applications, covering everything from astronomy to vector graphics.

Outside the United States, in countries such as Norway, Spain, Uruguay, and Brazil, regional and national deployments of completely open source workstations are common in schools.

Medium Profile: Moodle, LibreOffice, and Thin Client

Moodle is an open source learning (or course) management system that has seen explosive growth in popularity in U.S. schools and around the world. Hard numbers are difficult to come by, but it is probably number two in the U.S. K–12 learning management system market and climbing. Moodle's pedagogical approach is popular with many teachers, and it now supports a robust ecosystem of commercial providers of hosting, support, and training (for example, Moodlerooms, ClassroomRevolution, and Remote-Learner).

Switching from Microsoft Office to LibreOffice (www.docu mentfoundation.org/) is a change that many districts consider. LibreOffice is meant to be an open source alternative to Office and other office productivity suites, so it is easy to look at the budget line for MS Office licenses and wonder if it could be eliminated by using LibreOffice and spent elsewhere. The answer is "yes, but not necessarily easily," and the transition costs can be substantial.

Plan carefully, particularly with power users. Because LibreOffice can read MS Office files, you *do not* have to move everyone in the district at the same time. Migrating students and teachers while leaving secretaries, accountants, and others on MS Office can both save thousands of dollars and avoid the most difficult transition headaches.

"Thin client computing" uses simple, low-power, silent, solid state terminals connected to a powerful server instead of a network of full PCs. In the right context and with a skillful implementation, schools around the world have achieved stunning results through Linux-based thin clients (http://ltsp.org), gaining high reliability and substantial reductions in hardware and support costs as well as power consumption. How well a full or partial thin client deployment will work in a given situation is highly variable based on local expertise, network efficiency, and other factors. Thin clients are worthy of careful consideration as a component of your technology plan.

Low Profile: The Server Closet

As has been the case in business and industry, schools have been quietly running open source software in their server closet for years, often without "the suits" even knowing it. Open source software is strongest and most mature in this domain; virtually all server infrastructure can be migrated to prove robust enough for a corporation. Depending on the background and disposition of your IT staff and vendors, it might be the easiest, or the hardest, place to implement open source solutions.

NEXT STEPS

Once armed with a better understanding of free and open source software, here are some next steps that administrators can take.

Planning

Increasing the effective use of open source software within a school district cannot be done by edict or proclamation from administrators. It is a long process that must include your IT staff, vendors, teachers, and, ideally, students. You probably already have a process for doing strategic planning around technology. Make the long-term advantages of free and open source software a part of that conversation.

Training

Training will be a key part of this or any other major transition in technology deployments, for your IT staff and users. Train leaders first. Do frequent pilots and tests to monitor how much training will be necessary in full deployments. You might find unintuitive patterns—casual users may need little training for what seem like sweeping changes while power users may need very focused training and hand-holding for specific pain points.

Hiring

Update your technical job descriptions to include training and experience with relevant open source software.

Pilots and Testing

One of the great advantages of open source software is that you can easily do small tests and pilots with minimal cost or overhead. Take advantage of this.

Purchasing

You will be buying things in making the transition to free software. There is an ongoing bootstrapping problem in the market for services around free and open source software. Schools have trouble finding companies to offer service; interested companies have trouble finding customers. Make your intentions clear to current and prospective vendors.

Implementation

Don't rush it. Don't do the hard parts first. Pick low-hanging fruit, implement low-risk projects, and build confidence. It is not a race.

SUMMARY

Piecemeal adoption of free and open source software will continue to provide practical and educational benefits to teachers, students, parents, and taxpayers. However, what is truly exciting is the possibility of long-term fundamental changes in the way the educational technology market functions.

A predominantly open source ecosystem in educational technology would be based on vendors competing on quality of service instead of lock-in based on licensing and closed formats. Increasingly large-scale collaborations among schools, universities, and vendors would propagate innovation across the country instead of reinventing the wheel over and over in new proprietary packages. The K–12 educational technology market needs to become a science in the full Enlightenment sense: rational, transparent, and open for public debate, analysis, and critique. Only when we embrace software freedom will that truly happen.

References

Brodkin, J. (2007, September 20). *Open source impossible to avoid, Gartner says.* Network World. Retrieved from www.network world.com/news/2007/092007-open-source-unavoidable.html

GNU Operating System. (2011). *The free software definition.* Retrieved from www.gnu.org/philosophy/free-sw.html

Open Source Initiative. (2011). *The open source definition.* Retrieved from www.opensource.org/docs/osd

Saugus Union School District. (2011). SWATTEC (Student Writing Achievement Through Technology Enhanced Collaboration) project. Retrieved from http://community .sau gususd.org/swattec/

CHAPTER 9

Educational Gaming

John W. Rice

Once upon a time there was a nuclear laboratory named Brookhaven. In its heyday back in the 1950s, Brookhaven held an open house each year, during which time the general public was invited to tour the facilities and listen to nuclear engineers and scientists lecture about their work. The United States was in an arms race with the former Soviet Union, and the entire country was focused on educating students in the sciences as never before (or since).

Willy Higinbotham was in charge of equipment for Brookhaven. One year before open house, he got the brainy idea to attach a couple of paddlewheels to a computer and an oscilloscope. With a little programming, he created a simulated "tennis" game in which players could bounce a virtual ball over a net.

The first "video game" thus was born and it was a resounding success. People lined up in droves at the Brookhaven open house for a chance to play Higinbotham's new game, and it inspired future programmers to develop products like the first commercial video games, including Pong (Flatow, 1992).

Over the years, as video games moved from the laboratory to televisions and arcades, then to supercomputers and personal computers, educators have been fascinated by video games' educational potential. Could something that holds so much interest for the young be hijacked and used for pedagogical purposes?

The answer is yes, but not always in the way teachers hope. Video games are very good at "teaching" certain things but, as so many proposed panaceas, they are not always the best method to improve scores on standardized tests at the secondary level. They do fill an important niche in the educator's toolkit, and for certain lessons and training programs they are often the best tool for the job.

THE THREE Rs
OF INSTRUCTIONAL VIDEO GAMES

Whether administrators are considering implementation of instructional video games at the primary, secondary, or collegiate level, they should realize that video games have certain advantages for classroom use in general. We might call these the three Rs of instructional video games: repetition, reward, and reason.

Repetition

At the simplest level, video games can offer endless repetition of instructional elements for children in a fun and engaging way. We see this in many of the best games aimed at primary students involving word and letter recognition as well as simple arithmetic. In fact, math achievement at the primary levels has a long history of tested improvement when instruction is combined with an appropriate "skill and drill" video game (Randel, Morris, Wetzel, & Whitehill, 1992).

Games focusing more or less exclusively on repetitive elements typically are best aimed at the lower grade levels and can be played during class or lab time without concern regarding time restraints. They can be easily set aside until the following day or the next visit to the lab. They reinforce classroom instruction rather than replacing it and add a fun element to possibly tedious repetitive work.

Reward

Reward is a dominant motivator in digital worlds. It often is intangible and of little or no use in the real world. Sometimes the reward is as simple as a public posting of meritorious effort by a user: online forums may rank posters based on how many messages they have posted; purchase sites may publicly track users by how many items they have bought or books they have reviewed; and social sites may display the number of "friends" a user has accumulated.

Reward systems in games work along similar lines. They are highly abstract and often utterly useless outside the gaming environment, yet players will compete for them and diligently strive to earn them while playing. Sometimes the reward is as simple as a high score displayed publicly with the user name or player's initials. Sometimes the reward is virtual gold coins the player can use to purchase virtual items in the game. Sometimes the reward is special "clothing" or accessories worn by the player's avatar and only available after certain tasks are completed.

Regardless of the exact nature of the virtual rewards, they serve as powerful motivators to accomplish whatever is needed to earn them in the game. The public nature of the prize usually proffers bragging rights to the players, which enhances the reward's intrinsic value. This element of motivation has been observed since the early days of online multiuser game play (Bartle, 1996).

Most video games come with some sort of reward system built in, even if it is simply a record of high scores. Teachers can often incorporate the reward systems found in instructional video games into their classrooms, regardless of the games' complexity levels.

Reason

Advanced educational games are not the simple tennis simulations of Willy Higinbotham's day. Rather, they are complex and intellectually stimulating environments. The scientific method often is in full use, even in purely entertainment titles with no educational benefits deliberately programmed into the environment (Steinkuehler & Duncan, 2009).

Teamwork, collaborative problem-solving, and experiential education all are intangible areas where video game instruction shines. Most of all, the higher-level reasoning required to engage in these games creates environments in which abstract thought and the upper levels of Bloom's taxonomy can be put to good use within instructional frameworks (Rice, 2007).

CHOOSING GAMES FOR THE CLASSROOM

When providing leadership regarding teacher adoption of instructional video games for classroom use, administrators will find the following five considerations helpful. These questions are born out of experience in classroom implementation and are offered more as guiding questions rather than strict rules.

Does the game include built-in tracking and statistics? One of the key strengths of a good educational game is its ability to track student progress within the virtual environment. Teachers will not have time to track progress for each student so the game should do that for them. Many instructional games provide statistical feedback on the students as well, showing time spent in various areas online and highlighting objectives that were either met or proved troublesome. This will allow a teacher to intervene, for example, if a particular student spends too much time in one enjoyable location to the exclusion of other areas containing additional, as yet to be mastered, objectives.

Is the game prealigned to state standards? Video games designed specifically for school use will come prealigned to major state and national standards. One of the weaknesses when using off-the-shelf entertainment software in the classroom is that usually there are no curricular alignments included in the box. This means that if the program is integrated into a school's activities, someone will have to take the time to write the alignments. However, games created specifically for school use often will be written with major objectives in mind, and the creators will include a list of alignments to the appropriate standards.

Does the game train or teach? Training games are used heavily in the military and industry. Air traffic controllers, for instance, are trained extensively using video game technology (Wald, 2008). Because the focus at schools often is more aligned with academic content, games chosen for classroom inclusion typically should focus on teaching academic skills rather than work skills. Exceptions abound, of course, such as with life skills students or those in workforce programs.

Is the game time frame friendly? A typical instructional period may last forty-five minutes or so. If students must assemble in a classroom and then move to a computer lab, instructional time is even more limited. Many games can be stopped, with data saved, and later continued right where the players left off. Other games have objectives that require longer times to meet and cannot be stopped as easily or without disruption to the learning process. Longer games still can be used in school settings; however, their time frames might necessitate exclusive use in after-school or summer programs when the bell schedule is not so pressing.

Is the game customizable by the teacher? Every teacher is different and many may want to include specific local or personal items within their instruction. Whether a teacher can customize a game—and how much time and effort is needed to perform the customization—may influence a committee's consideration of various titles. On the flip side, some administrators may not want teachers to vary from a set curriculum or objectives within a game if they are perfectly aligned to existing standards. Pilot-testing specific titles before widespread adoption remains a good idea and often will help answer this question to the satisfaction of all stakeholders involved.

OBTAINING GAMES FOR THE CLASSROOM

So where do teachers obtain these fabulous educational games that have students playing for a pedagogical purpose? Generally, teachers may modify off-the-shelf software to suit their educational needs. We see this with the many modifications of the *Civilization* game series for history and social studies or with simple changes to the language settings in *The Sims* to provide an immersive second-language environment for students. New titles are released monthly, so sometimes older titles have been modified by teachers more than newer titles. An added bonus for older titles: any video game over six months old is usually far less expensive at retail.

Alternatively, teachers and their students can download or play online one of the many university-developed educational games. These are usually produced with funding from grants through government agencies such as the National Science Foundation, the National Aeronautics and Space Administration (NASA), and the National Endowment for the Arts. Many fine products have been tailored to meet state and national standards in the classroom through government funding. Thanks to their public development grants, these games are typically free to use, although some might require teacher training before classroom implementation by the host university is allowed.

Some examples of these vibrant, advanced instructional games include *Quest Atlantis* at Indiana University, which focuses on persuasive writing and the sciences; *Path of the Elders*, created by the Canadian government to teach the history and culture of the Mushkegowuk and Anishinaabe peoples in Ontario; and *Selene*, a video game centered on lunar science, funded by NASA and hosted by Wheeling Jesuit University.

Finally, schools can purchase games designed specifically for classroom use. Two good examples for high school include Tabula

Digita's *DimensionM*, which focuses on math skills in an advanced immersive gaming environment, and Brigham Young University's *Virtual ChemLab*, which is sold through Pearson and uses video game technologies to simulate a complete working chemistry laboratory.

SUMMARY

Instructional video games can be a vibrant and powerful tool in the classroom. If administrators and teachers are aware ahead of time of a particular title's strengths and weaknesses, they will be better prepared to fully leverage the game in their particular instructional settings.

Similar to other instructional tools, video games are no panacea and never will provide the ultimate method to create higher test scores. However, when properly used they may help students to increase specific skills, academic and otherwise. For basic skills, video games excel while tirelessly providing a fun environment for student practice. For the intangible elements often lacking in formal education, video games offer strong potential in areas such as cooperative problem-solving, teamwork, providing a sense of self-worth, realizing the importance of differing viewpoints and cultures, and many other fuzzy areas not usually tested on standardized exams. For the hard sciences, video games are exceptionally powerful when providing experiential learning and can provide virtual simulative environments that students can explore without the fear surrounding real life hazards.

Most of all, video games are fun. Properly included in the classroom and combined with good instruction, they offer a way for students to learn in an engaging and exciting environment.

References
Bartle, R. A. (1996). Hearts, clubs, diamonds, spades: Players who suit MUDs. *Journal of MUD Research, 1*(1).

Flatow, I. (1992). *They all laughed . . . From light bulbs to lasers: The fascinating stories behind the great inventions that have changed our lives.* New York: HarperCollins.

Randel, J. M., Morris, B. A., Wetzel, C. D., & Whitehill, B. V. (1992). The effectiveness of games for educational purposes: A review of recent research. *Simulation & Gaming, 23,* 261–276.

Rice, J. W. (2007). Assessing higher order thinking in video games. *Journal of Technology and Teacher Education, 15*(1), 87–100.

Steinkuehler, C., & Duncan, S. (2009). Informal scientific reasoning in online virtual worlds. *Journal of Science Education & Technology.* DOI: 10.1007/s10956–008–9120–8.

Wald, M. L. (2008, October 7). For air traffic trainees, games with a serious purpose. *New York Times.* Retrieved from www .nytimes.com/2008/10/08/us/08controller .html?pagewanted=1&_ r=2&sq=serious%20game&st=cse&scp=1

CHAPTER 10

Social Bookmarking

Dean Shareski

and Mary Beth Hertz

You open your e-mail and see a great link that your colleague or friend sent you. A Facebook friend posts an interesting link. You come across an important article while reading the *New York Times* or catch a terrific resource posted on Twitter. How do you keep track of all of these resources from so many different places? What's the best way to share them with others? How can you share multiple sites and resources with your staff and students?

Do you mark all of these sites as "favorites" using your browser's built-in bookmarks or favorites tool? If so, what do you do when you want to access the sites from home, work, a friend's house, or on the road?

HOW DOES SOCIAL BOOKMARKING WORK?

Social bookmarking allows you to share your favorite links and bookmarks with your friends and colleagues. It also allows you to keep all of your favorite links in one place so that you can access them from any computer that has an Internet connection. Social bookmarking offers a wonderful solution to the issues raised previously and also opens up opportunities to do even more. Social bookmarking has numerous implications for professional, personal, and classroom use.

Social bookmarking starts with choosing a service that will help you gather resources and make them easily accessible and shareable with others. One of the most popular bookmarking services is Delicious (www.delicious.com). For educators, Diigo (www.diigo .com) is gaining in popularity because of some features that are geared toward classroom teachers. We also are seeing a shift toward technologies such as Evernote (www.evernote.com), although not specifically classified as social bookmarking tools, that are being modified by users to do similar things.

No matter which tool you choose, the first step after saving a website is to decide how you want to categorize it for easy retrieval later. Once your library starts to fill up, it can become hard to find a link that was saved months earlier. Using keywords or tags helps with this task; for instance, tagging a bookmark with a keyword such as *Web 2.0* for a site about Web 2.0 tools will help you find it later. To assist you, the service you choose likely will offer you either a toolbar or bookmarklet that you can easily add to your browser. In most cases, the toolbar will require an installation, whereas the bookmarklet is no different than adding a favorite or bookmark as you would for any other website. The other difference is that usually the toolbar add-on offers you more features. In districts where installation of software is prohibited, the bookmarklet offers a nice alternative.

EXAMPLES OF USE

Social bookmarking can be a powerful tool for staff members in a school or district to share resources; collaborate around an article, blog post, or other online resource; or keep up with new trends in education.

Individuals can use social bookmarking to collect resources and tag and organize them in a variety of ways. The social aspect means that you can easily find others' resources and quickly see if they are looking for similar things that you are. If several like-minded individuals all are searching and vetting resources, this can save you time and introduce you to ideas and resources that you might not otherwise have discovered. The sites that you save can be shared or kept private. Educators often use social bookmarking sites for professional use and gladly share those, but they also may choose to keep personal sites such as vacation spots or hobbies private because they know other educators are interested only in their professional sites.

Professionals and staff members might actively create special, easily recognized tags that are specific to their work or subject area in order to collect resources. For example, using the tag "5thgrade-science" might enable teachers of a similar grade and subject to collect resources and share them with a single URL or website address. In most cases, social bookmarking services offer "widgets" that can be embedded on websites or blogs. For instance, a school may choose to display resources for parents on Internet safety on its website. A simple widget allows the school to display a dynamic list of updated sites based on a specific tag or user.

Students also can benefit from these tools for research and collaboration. Teachers can easily monitor and follow student progress on projects. Teachers who are using social bookmarking tools with students should choose a tool that allows for easy account creation. For elementary age students, this might mean an account that allows a teacher to create accounts for students without an e-mail address. For older students or in schools that allow for student e-mail accounts, make sure that the sign-up process doesn't require any personal or identifying information.

Use of social bookmarking tools can make group projects easier for students and teachers to monitor. Students can share resources with each other as well as, depending on the tool, notes and highlights. Social bookmarking puts students behind the wheel in the information-gathering process for a project or assignment, or when exploring a question. Teachers also can track a student's progress in collecting resources and address any misconceptions or faulty resources.

The resources that a student or student group collects and shares using social bookmarking tools don't disappear once the class, lesson, or project is over. Students can begin to build a comprehensive library of resources that they can take with them and even add to later.

WHY DOES SOCIAL BOOKMARKING MATTER?

Social bookmarking might be the easiest way to experience networking while selfishly collecting and arranging resources to suit your personal needs. Knowing that others have decided to tag a site increases the likelihood that the site is of value. With the advent of sites such as Twitter, we're beginning to realize the power of people-oriented searches. Social bookmarking sites offer exactly that: the ability to tap into the knowledge of others. Finding other individuals who are interested in similar things can lead educators to richer connections beyond shared use of the social bookmarking service.

Even if you don't have your own account, you can use social bookmarking tools to subscribe to RSS feeds from individuals or from tags. Again, the power of vetted resources means that your research is likely to be more useful than a Google search. Rather than searching for that really useful resource over and over, you can save it to your "library in the cloud." Tags and RSS feeds bring information right to you without the time-consuming, repetitive searching of resources all over the web.

WHICH TOOL SHOULD I USE?

Here is a comparison of three social bookmarking tools currently available. Please note that, due to the ever-changing nature of the web, these tools may change or no longer exist when this book goes to print.

Tool	Student e-mail required	Create a profile	Browser add-on	Bundle sites	View bookmarked sites within the tool itself	E-mail bundles or sites	RSS feed for links	Highlighting and note taking
Delicious	yes	no	yes	yes	no	no	yes	no
Diigo	no	yes	yes	yes	yes	yes	yes	yes
Evernote	yes	no	yes	yes	yes	yes	no	yes

SUMMARY

No matter what tool you use, social bookmarking offers you portability, share-ability, and quality resources not always found in a typical Google search. The ability to customize this experience means that information is much more malleable and meaningful. Social bookmarking often is a gateway tool for people to move more deeply into the use of social media as a learning vehicle.

CHAPTER 11

Online Mind Mapping

Carl Anderson

and Richard Byrne

Mind mapping is a way of making your thoughts visual through the use of charts, graphs, graphic organizers, and timelines. Whether it is being used for instruction or for collaborative work, mind mapping allows learners to process complex and dynamic thoughts or concepts. Mind mapping also provides an efficient means of communicating those ideas to others. The benefit of the mind-mapping tools that are online is that you can create a permanent and portable version of those visuals. By making the record portable and accessible, online participants in a brainstorming session can work from multiple locations on the same project. For example, students who are physically absent from the classroom still can contribute to a brainstorming session. Collaborative online mind-mapping tools also provide online educators with an effective instructional strategy usually best employed in face-to-face learning environments. Using a free online tool for mind mapping, such as Mind42 (www.Mind42.com) or Bubbl.us (www .bubbl.us), also affords the authors of the mind map the option to publish their work and share it with vast audiences on the Internet.

MIND MAPPING
AS AN INSTRUCTIONAL STRATEGY

Visual tools such as mind maps or graphic organizers are important for visual learners. They help learners create visual connections among facts, thoughts, and concepts. They allow for visual manipulation of thought patterns and sequences. Through the use of shape, color, and form, concepts and terms can be efficiently coded and organized, allowing for ease of associations. Boxtel, Linden, Roelofs, and Erkens (2002) explained that concept mapping helps learners reflect on their own understanding and empowers them to construct their own knowledge and meaning. Collaborative concept mapping also can be a powerful method of initiating student dialogue.

Mind-mapping and concept-mapping activities can be used as an active learning strategy. Active learning strategies are instructional methods that promote the use of higher-order thinking, metacognition, and participation in the active processing of content or construction of knowledge. By employing the use of active learning strategies, the instructor assumes that learning is by nature an active endeavor (McKinney, 2010) and that different people learn in different ways (Meyers & Jones, 1993, as cited by McKinney, 2010). To engage learners in active learning involves having them do things while thinking about what they are doing (Bonwell & Eison, 1991). In the process, students are mindfully engaged.

The use of mind mapping and concept mapping as an instructional strategy is not unique to the twenty-first century. In the past, a common mind-mapping practice called for instructors to provide a template for a topic that their students then filled in. Chacón (2003) referred to the use of mind mapping in that manner as creating learning containers. When this process is moved to the web, these online learning containers, once filled, can be altered by addition or subtraction, which can reflect new learning or the streamlining of knowledge.

Collaborative, online mind mapping allows students to voice their opinions, support their ideas, and see other points of view. One framework for this process calls for instructors to simply provide students with a blank slate on which they share their thoughts (Budd, 2004). Budd argued that this framework for mind mapping can increase student confidence and described a process in which he provided his students with sticky notes on which they recorded their ideas. After one hour, his students posted their notes to a bulletin board. The bulletin board of sticky notes was then used for a discussion. Budd encouraged students to incorporate colors and small drawings as prompts and organizational aids. Finally, Budd emphasized the need for instructors to provide informal feedback during the process by addressing questions directly to the more passive members of the group (Budd, 2004).

LIMITATIONS OF ANALOG MIND MAPPING

There are three limitations to the process described by Budd that can be eliminated through the use of web-based tools such as Wallwisher (www.wallwisher.com). Wallwisher is a free, web-based program that allows instructors to create an online bulletin board on which students can add sticky notes that consist of up to 160 characters of text, hyperlinks, images, and videos. The process that Budd described is an analog process that requires all students to be in the same physical location to participate in the process. Through the use of Wallwisher, students who are not physically present in the same classroom—or who are participating at a different time—can contribute to the mind-mapping session. Budd's process also limits students to the use of pencil and paper in diagramming their ideas. Wallwisher allows participants in a mind-mapping session to include and reference photographs and videos to help them fully explain and support their ideas. Finally, archiving the ideas shared by participants in Budd's process requires either the instructor or the students to maintain a physical file of the sticky notes.

Although this may not be a concern when working with older students, it is a very real concern for many K–12 classroom teachers. Wallwisher and other online mind-mapping services maintain an archive of all of the students' sticky notes, which then can be accessed at any time by the instructor. This archive allows instructors to make informal assessments of students' knowledge and ideas not only during the mind-mapping process but also with reflection after the process has been completed. Here are some specific teaching activities that take advantage of the affordances offered by online mind-mapping tools.

Teaching Activities Using Online Mind-Mapping Tools	
Activity	Tools
Online Know, Want, Learn chart • Students share facts, ideas, and questions. As the wall fills up, students who know the answers to others' questions post those answers. Drag items from "want" to "know." Students move notes into sequence.	Board800 CoSketch Dabbleboard Edistorm FlockDraw Linoit Nota Postica ShowDocument Sneffel Spaaze Stixy Twiddla Wallwisher
Exit cards for student or attendee feedback • Teacher provides a space for students to post feedback about what they liked and did not like about class. • Meeting or event facilitator provides a space for attendees to post feedback about what they liked and did not like about the meeting or event.	Creately Dabbleboard Edistorm Scriblink Twiddla Wallwisher

Construct concept maps • Students or teachers place a main concept in the center of the screen. Students then write supporting facts and evidence around the central concept. Students arrange the supporting facts and evidence to show the connections between them in their support of the central concept.	Board800 Bubbl Cacoo CoSketch Ekpenso FlockDraw Mapul Mind42 MindMeister Slatebox SlickPlan Think Wisemapping
Create causation charts • Students place a significant event, such as WWII, on the screen. Students then write events and concepts contributing to the cause of the central event.	Creately Dabbleboard Ekpenso Google Docs Mapul Mind42 Scriblink ShowDocument SlickPlan SpicyNodes Think Twiddla
Analyze fiction literature • During or after reading, students identify the main idea. Students use branches and smaller boxes or bubbles on screen to identify supporting details, subplots, and characters.	Board800 Bubbl Cacoo Ekpenso Flockdraw Gliffy Mapul Mind42 SlickPlan Think Wisemapping

(continued)

Activity	Tools
Analyze nonfiction literature • Similar in style to analyzing fiction literature. Students record supporting details but also identify what they perceive as unanswered questions or flaws in the author's argument(s).	Bubbl Cacoo Edistorm Flockdraw Linoit Wallwisher
Create timelines • Students create multimedia timelines to trace the history of a specific topic or event.	Capzles Dipity OurStory Timeglider TimeRime Timetoast xtimeline
Visualize complex systems • Students create flow charts to illustrate how a complex system such as a computer program, electronic circuit, government system, economic system, or biological system works.	Creately DropMind Flowchart Gliffy Lovely Charts LucidChart Mapul SlickPlan Text2Mindmap Webspiration
Prewriting activity • Students can create mind maps to organize their thoughts around a topic for either creative or formal writing.	Bubbl Cacoo Edistorm Ekpenso Flockdraw Linoit Mapul Mind42 SlickPlan SpicyNodes Text2Mindmap Think Wallwisher

USING MIND-MAPPING TOOLS AS AN ADMINISTRATOR

Although online mind-mapping tools can be powerful for learners in a classroom, they also can be powerful additions to the school administrator's tool belt. Mind-mapping tools can enhance brainstorming sessions at staff meetings, producing an editable document that lives on beyond the meeting. Through the use of collaborative mind maps, work can continue long after the meeting when students or staff are most ready to work with it. Online mind mapping also can be used as a great communication tool. For example, imagine that your organization is going to enact a complex calling system for disseminating important emergency information to staff. This system might not be easily communicated verbally or with written text, especially if your organization is large, but having a visual method to convey this information can make the complex seem simple. Some of these tools can be effectively used to get feedback from people. Often we don't hear what we need to hear in faculty meetings because people are afraid to say what is truly on their mind or there is not time to hear everyone's concerns. Having a collaborative mind-mapping tool can allow people the ability to give anonymous feedback and thus help facilitate organizational change.

SUMMARY

Mind mapping is a powerful format in which students can visualize and manipulate information. Online mind-mapping tools provide teachers and students with flexible platforms for sharing thoughts, developing ideas, and synthesizing information in a visual format. Research supports the concept of mind mapping as a powerful teaching and learning strategy. The flexibility of online mind-mapping tools enhances that proved strategy.

References

Bonwell, C. C., & Eison, J. A. (1991). *Active learning: Creating excitement in the classroom*. The National Teaching & Learning Forum. Retrieved from www.ntlf.com/html/lib/bib/91-9dig.htm

Boxtel, C., Linden, J., Roelofs, E., & Erkens, G. (2002). Collaborative concept mapping: Provoking and supporting meaningful discourse. *Theory into Practice, 41*(1), 40–46.

Budd, J. W. (2004). Mind maps as classroom exercises. *The Journal of Economic Education, 35*(1), 35–46.

Chacón, F. (2003). *Mind-mapping for web instruction and learning*. The Convergence of Learning & Technology, Ohio Learning Network. Retrieved from www.oln.org/conferences/OLN2003/papers/FUS_Chacon.pdf

McKinney, K. (2010). *Active learning*. Center for Teaching, Learning, and Technology. Retrieved from www.cat.ilstu.edu/additional/tips/newActive.php

Additional Resources

Abi-El-Mona, I., & Adb-El-Khalick, F. (2008). The influence of mind mapping on eighth graders' science achievement. *School Science and Mathematics, 108*(7), 298–312.

Al-Jarf, R. (2009). *Enhancing freshman students' writing skills with a mind mapping software*. Paper presented at the Fifth International Scientific Conference, eLearning, and Software for Education, Bucharest, April.

Belcher, J. (2000–2003). *Technology enabled active learning (TEAL)*. Retrieved from http://icampus.mit.edu/projects/TEAL.shtml

Buzan, T., & Buzan, B. (1994). *The mind map book: How to use radiant thinking to maximize your brains untapped potential*. New York: Dutton.

Garcia, G.N.A. (2010, March 24). *Mapping the gap with concept maps*. Bridging the gap. Retrieved from http://researchtopractice.word press.com/2010/03/24/bridging-the-gaps-with-concept-maps

Goodnough, K., & Long, R. (2002). Mind mapping: A graphic organizer for the pedagogical toolbox. *Science Scope, 25*(8), 20–24.

Goodnough, K., & Woods, R. (2002). *Student and teacher perceptions of mind mapping: A middle school case study.* Paper presented at the Annual Meeting of American Educational Research Association, New Orleans, April 1–5.

Harmin, M. (1994). *Inspiring active learning: A handbook for teachers.* Alexandria, VA: ASCD.

Holland, B., Holland, L., & Davies, J. (2003/2004). An investigation into the concept of mind mapping and the use of mind mapping software to support and improve student academic performance. *Learning and Teaching Projects 2003/2004*, pp. 89–94.

Kenyon, G. (2002, April). Mind mapping can help dyslexics. *BBC News Online.* Retrieved from http://news.bbc.co.uk/2/hi/uk_news/education/1926739.stm

The Ohio Learning Network. (n.d.). *Use active learning techniques.* Retrieved from www.oln.org/ILT/7_principles/active.php

Marzano, R. J., Norford, J. S., Payneter, D. E., Pickering, D. J., & Gaddy, B. B. (2001). *A handbook for classroom instruction that works.* Alexandria, VA: ASCD.

Marzano, R. J., Pickering, D. J., & Pollock, J. E. (2001). *Classroom instruction that works: Research-based strategies for increasing student achievement.* Alexandria, VA: ASCD.

National Research Council. (2000). *How people learn: Brain, mind, experience, and school.* Washington, DC: National Academy Press.

Paykoç, F., Mengi, B., Kamay, P. O., Onkol, P., Ozgur, B., Pilli, O., & Yildirim, H. (2004). *What are the major curriculum issues? The use of mind mapping as a brainstorming exercise.* Paper presented at the First International Conference on Concept Mapping, Pamplona, Spain.

Sandholtz, J. H., Ringstaff, C., & Dwyer, D. C. (1997). *Teaching with technology creating student-centered classrooms.* New York: Teachers College Press.

Silberman, M. (1996). *Active learning: 101 strategies to teach any subject.* Boston: Allyn & Bacon.

Tileston, D. W. (2007). *Teaching strategies for active learning: Five essentials for your teaching plan.* Thousand Oaks, CA: Corwin Press.

University of Michigan Center for Research on Learning and Teaching. (2009). *Teaching strategies: Active and collaborative learning.* Retrieved from www.crlt.umich.edu/tstrategies/tsal.php

University of Minnesota Center for Teaching and Learning. (2008, May). *Twelve active learning strategies.* Retrieved from www1.umn.edu/ohr/teachlearn/tutorials/powerpoint/learning/index.html

Wycoff, J. (1991). *Mindmapping: Your personal guide to exploring creativity and problem-solving.* New York: Berkley Books.

CHAPTER 12

Course Management Systems

Scott S. Floyd and Miguel Guhlin

"How can we conduct campuswide professional learning for our teachers," asked Joanelda, a veteran principal in a large urban school district, "that doesn't end when the bell rings at 3:00 PM?" A course management system (CMS) makes it possible for K–12 and adult learners to keep learning after the school bell rings. A CMS is an online learning facilitation and delivery system that combines text, video, and other forms of content in a protected environment. Some systems in use now include Moodle (http://moodle.com), recently adopted by PBS TeacherLine and in use internationally; Sakai (www.sakaiproject.org) used in higher education; and Blackboard (www.blackboard.com), a commercial CMS.

AFTER THE SCHOOL BELL RINGS

Facilitating sustained professional learning opportunities for teachers is a challenge for K–12 school districts. Some of the most common ways course management systems are used include the following:

- Online professional learning communities for educators that extend existing face-to-face structures

- Classroom communities that include safe, virtual spaces for students, teachers, and parents to interact around student work

- Parental outreach programs that facilitate opportunities for positive dialogue among parents, administrators, and teachers

Each of these applications of course management systems can enhance educators' school cultures and K–16 instructional settings.

ONLINE PROFESSIONAL LEARNING COMMUNITIES

"How can I facilitate a book study that all my staff can participate in?" asked a principal who had just read a book on the superintendent's reading list and wanted to have a discussion about it with his teachers. Time for teachers during the day was short due to high-stakes testing, parent conferences, paperwork, lesson planning, and more. Although there were rich media resources available that he could use to kick-start the conversation, the principal was unsure how to organize them and create an interactive learning environment. This is where a course management system such as Moodle comes in handy. Moodle, a free open source solution available at no cost, was designed to facilitate K–16 and adult online learning. Martin Dougiamas developed Moodle to meet the needs of teachers and students at a time when available learning tools were severely limited. Moodle supporters and developers—a global community of enthusiasts contributing in their respective areas of expertise, programming to training—have expanded Moodle far beyond his original vision, exemplifying the spirit of free software.

In this situation, an instructional leader's role shifts to a facilitator of online learning for education professionals. This approach is critical in working toward "advocating, nurturing, and sustaining a school culture and instructional program conducive to student learning and staff professional growth" (Council of Chief State School Officers, 2008, p. 18). It is an expectation echoed by the National Education Technology Standards for Administrators (NETS·A).

Collecting just-in-time survey data can be simplified through use of a course management system. Questionnaire, quiz, or survey modules enable you to create a short questionnaire that staff complete; the information then is displayed in graphical format. This can make school climate surveys, parent satisfaction, and customer service data collection easier and more transparent to all stakeholders. Essentially, a CMS can be used to build an online learning community that protects your conversations behind a user name and password, valuable when you want some resources kept "inside" for staff and student use.

CLASSROOM COMMUNITIES

Safe learning environments are one of the reasons leaders adopt a CMS for organizational and instructional use. Staff, students, and even parents have to log on to the CMS to access its content. This makes CMSs the tool of choice for many classroom teachers who prefer a "walled garden" where students can learn in safety while teachers and administrators monitor and support instruction. Parents can be invited in with limited access. The abilities to hold conversations in forums prior to completing a task, turn in assignments, and complete quizzes that get graded and placed in the CMS's built-in grade book all make the CMS a coveted digital assistant. Publishing through embedded media (video, slideshows, audio files, and so on) within the CMS also allows leaders to gain feedback from peers and teachers. This prepares them for the increasingly transparent world ahead in which publishing to the masses is an expectation and not an exception.

PARENT OUTREACH PROGRAMS

"Parents wish to be more engaged by schools," shares a recent report, "but need better tools and information" (Bridgeland, Dilulio, Streeter, & Mason, 2008, p. 3). If you are a principal, superintendent, or head of school, you realize that parents are more connected—via netbooks, laptops, mobile phones, and other devices—than ever before. Although having a morning coffee session is still important, it is not enough to reach the wide audience of parents in your school who may be unable to be present because they have to go to work early or are working two or more jobs that occupy their time. If you can put your message online, however, you enable them to connect—and respond—to your message. They then can follow what you, their children, their children's teacher, and their peers have to say because they can subscribe to the content being presented. In course management systems such as Moodle or Blackboard, parents can pull the content they need when they want it, whether it's an e-mail to their in-box or via subscription through an RSS feed.

Moodle and other course management systems offers one-stop sharing of audio and video podcasts of children in a safe, controlled, yet engaging environment. Engaging with authentic learning via a CMS allows parents to see what is happening in the school.

MOODLE MODULES
THAT BUILD COMMUNITY

Moodle modules that enhance community include the following:

- Questionnaire activity module: Enables quick and easy survey creation

- WiziQ: Facilitates live interaction between facilitator and community members
- Activity podcast: Makes it easy to create and share audio recordings as podcasts
- iPodcast: Enables one to share podcasts via iTunes
- Twitter block: Allows for Moodle users to update their Twitter status from within Moodle
- Facebook: Enables Facebook-Moodle integration for easy account log-in using Facebook accounts as the source
- Kaltura video: Makes it easy to host your own video using Kaltura, then place video in Moodle
- Google Apps for Education integration for Moodle: Makes it easy for students in your school system who have Moodle accounts to log on to Google Apps and seamlessly go back and forth between the two systems, gaining the benefits of both

For a more complete list of modules and sample school sites using course management systems, be sure to visit the free online educator resource Moodle Mayhem (http://moodlemayhem.org).

SUMMARY

Course management systems bring your vision of online professional development and safe e-learning environments to life. With the right attitude, you can turn any virtual space into your organization's learning space—not only for staff but also for students and parents. Course management systems enliven the void of virtual space, connecting the gap between sparks of thought. They do so because they enable us to juxtapose ourselves and our ideas in ways that can be harnessed for learning and growth. They allow us to make known the fireflies of individual ideas and capture them in a glass jar for study and illumination. Embrace course management systems when learning and collaboration must go hand in hand.

References

Bridgeland, J. M., Dilulio, J. J., Streeter, R. T., & Mason, J. (2008, October). *One dream, two realities: Perspectives of parents on two realities.* Civic Enterprises. Retrieved from www.civicenterprises .net/pdfs/onedream.pdf

Council of Chief State School Officers. (2008). *Educational leadership policy standards.* Washington, DC: Author.

See Sally Research: Evolving Notions of Information Literacy

Joyce Kasman Valenza and Doug Johnson

Digital and ubiquitous sources of information, expanded definitions of literacy and audience, and greater emphasis on creative problem-solving have dramatically changed how—and why—students "do" research. The following scenarios scan the evolution of the information and communication landscapes, sharing the new possibilities for student research.

1989 (preweb)

Sally Madonna is a high school junior very interested in environmental issues. The learning emphasis at her high school is on "research skills" (the first edition of the American Association of School Librarians' [AASL's] *Information Power* was published in 1988; it defined the role of the school library in the school and school librarians use it as an information literacy bible).

Development of Question

When the opportunity arises to research a controversial issue, Sally eagerly proposes an investigation of the environmental impact of the recent Exxon Valdez oil spill. The assignment calls for simple reporting at Bloom's knowledge and comprehension level because the major learning outcome is knowing how to write a "term paper." Sally may not have had much choice in her topic, considering the general lack of resources available in the average school or public library. Sally is asked to develop a "thesis" statement and to provide evidence that supports it.

Finding Resources

With her social studies teacher, Sally visits the high school library. In the library, the class uses the wooden library catalog with its drawers and paper cards to locate books. She consults the *Readers' Guide to Periodical Literature* and the vertical file for magazines in the stacks and newspaper clippings. Additionally, the librarian suggests the microfiche and CD-ROM collections for finding magazine articles. Although personal computers are coming into the schools through libraries and labs, electronic information sources are very much limited to reference materials such as encyclopedias on CDs with content that is simply the electronic version of the print editions.

Sally's librarian created a bibliography of resources and pulled a cart of materials related to controversial issues, but Sally finds very little material that gives her more than a simple background on critical environment issues. The librarian offers a ten-minute introduction to possible sources. Because this is the first major environmental event of its type, Sally knows that books specific to this oil spill may not be available. The librarian can connect to a service called *Dialog* with a dial-up modem, but this is an expensive service that cannot really be scaled out for an entire school and most students haven't even connected yet to a specific topic or thesis. At the end of the period, the librarian reminds the class to grab a reference style-sheet handout.

When she gets home, Sally asks Mom and Dad if she can have the car to visit the public library and searches the house for change for the copy machine.

At the public library, Sally fills in call slips and waits for help to retrieve recent issues of *Time* and *Newsweek* from the stacks and background articles on microfilm. Sally looks for both popular news and scholarly sources for background and gathers a nice collection of journals and newspapers. She has to visually scan the library's small collection of newspapers for any breaking news on the story.

Evaluation

Because the resources available to Sally have been selected by professional librarians, little time needs to be spent in the evaluation of credibility of the material. Traditionally, credentialed authors and reliable publishing houses are the hallmarks of a carefully developed library collection. Sally realizes that she is going to have to work hard to ensure that her resources on this breaking story are as current as possible. Her reference list is going to contain far more background material than new content and she is concerned.

Organization and Synthesis

Sally uses note cards to gather information about her topic and then organizes her information in an outline form. When she is ready, she writes in the expository voice, maintaining a carefully objective point of view.

Documentation

Having diligently kept track of her sources on index cards, Sally spends a large amount of time on a bibliography that conforms to specifics of MLA citation style. Each element of the source is in its proper place and each punctuation mark is carefully checked and rechecked. Sally's bibliography and endnotes will be heavily weighted in the final grade.

Communication

Sally's final product is an eight- to ten-page typewritten "report" that is read only by the teacher. Sally may save the paper but she is not keeping a formal portfolio of her academic work.

Final Grade

A for content and A- for mechanics (fewer than two errors per page)

2005 (Web 1.0)

Sally Spears is a high school junior very interested in environmental issues. The learning emphasis at her high school is on "information literacy." The Big6 information literacy process and similar state-designed models provide Sally's library media specialist the framework for assignments. So too does the second edition of AASL's and the Association of Educational Communications and Technology's (AECT's) *Information Power* (1998), with its information literacy standards and new emphasis on technology and partnerships for learning. The International Society for Technology in Education (ISTE) also has released its first set of National Educational Technology Standards (NETS) for technology literacy for students, teachers, and administrators. Its six categories of proficiency are basic operations and concepts; social, ethical, and human issues of technology use; productivity tools; communication tools; research tools; and problem-solving and decision-making tools.

Development of Question

When the opportunity arises to research a controversial issue, Sally eagerly proposes an investigation of the environmental impact of the recent Hurricane Katrina. Given the huge number of resources now available via the web and powerful new search engines, Sally has to carefully narrow the focus of her research by asking a specific question about her topic: "Would the restoration of coastal wetlands mitigate the impact of future Katrina-like storms in the Gulf?" Sally does some "pre-searching" to determine the resources available to her using Google and Wikipedia.

Finding Resources

While Sally begins her search using Google and Wikipedia, she realizes that her high school library website includes a number of databases that offer news and other documents. Her media specialist is beginning to create online pathfinders to guide Sally in her research. The media specialist discusses possible sources with the class, reminding students of several magazine and newspaper databases that offer access to current issues. The media specialist shows Sally how to use the advanced search features in Google to refine her search, to search the "hidden web," and to use subject-specific search engines. She reminds the whole class to take home a list of database passwords. Sally is both excited about and a little frustrated by the sheer number of possible information sources available to her.

Evaluation

Sally recognizes that there is a real need for her to evaluate her sources using reliable criteria and to be able to defend the reliability of the resources that she chooses. She realizes that database searches likely will yield the types of sources her teacher wants to see in her list of works cited. But Sally wonders if there is a way to connect with people who are on the ground. She uses e-mail to contact a wetlands expert in Florida for his perspective on the issue and awaits a response.

Organization and Synthesis

Sally's media specialist recently introduced the commercial online citation generator NoodleTools as a strategy for managing sources and documenting her work. Sally has to cite not just books and periodical articles but also websites, e-mail, and electronic reference materials. She takes advantage of the outlining and formatting tools built into her word processing program while she is writing the required drafts of her paper.

Communication

Sally is required to word process her document and to submit at least two drafts to her teacher before turning in the final project. A part of her assignment is to develop a PowerPoint presentation to accompany an oral report to her class about her findings. Sally's media specialist is instrumental in helping her import graphics and a video clip into the slideshow and suggests design strategies for effectively combining bullet points and graphics.

Sally stores an electronic copy of her paper on a 3.5-inch disk along with her personal printout and shares it with her teacher. She rehearses and tries to present looking at her audience—the class—without reading from her slides.

Final Grade
A for content, A- for mechanics, A+ for formatting, and A+ for her slide show

2010 (Web 2.0—Social Web)
Sally Gaga is a high school junior very interested in environmental issues. The learning emphasis at her high school is on developing "information and media fluency." The new information landscape is participatory. School libraries are playing a growing role in what is now being called *transliteracy*, the ability to read, write, and interact across a range of platforms, tools, and media. Those involved in Sally's learning life are influenced by ISTE's NETS Refreshed—with their new focus on creativity and innovation, communication and collaboration, research and information fluency, critical thinking, and digital citizenship—and AASL's *Standards for the 21st Century Learner*, which focus on inquiry, critical thinking, creating new knowledge, personal growth, and participating ethically and productively as members of our democratic society. Those who are helping Sally to learn and grow are far more connected to each other through their intersecting professional learning networks, which include their blogs, tweets, Nings, other social networks, and easy shared access to current research across disciplines. Credibility for Sally's educators' ideas now comes from application in the field as opposed to any single authoritative source or organization.

Development of Question

When the opportunity arises to research a controversial issue, Sally eagerly proposes an investigation of the environmental impact of the recent BP Gulf oil spill. The teacher encourages Sally to explore a dimension of this event that resonates personally with her. Sally one day hopes to run her own restaurant and she chooses to study the impact that the spill will have on seafood availability.

Sally is in the habit of setting up a research wiki to share her progress with her classroom teacher, her teacher-librarian, and her fellow students who will help peer edit and review her work.

Finding Resources

The students in Sally's one-to-one classroom begin their research on their classroom laptops. Sally's teacher-librarian worked with her teacher to create a pathfinder for hot issues research. The librarian drops in to give the class opening guidance and to remind learners of some newer search options. Sally checks the online catalog to locate print, e-books, and a variety of relevant media. She knows about Google's newer features such as Wonder Wheel and Timeline. She embeds some of the e-books she finds on Google Books on her research wiki. Sally also seeks video information in her search. She finds video news to be an excellent starting point for developing background knowledge and vocabulary around the issue. She grabs links for relevant videos and, when she can, embeds those too for easy access.

Sally knows that scholarly content will add power to her argument. After visiting databases the teacher-librarian recommends on the library's website, Sally sets up e-mail alerts and RSS feeds so that new content is pushed to both her e-mail in-box and the RSS reader that she has set up in her research wiki. Rather than revisiting Google day after day, after establishing search terms and tags she sets up alerts there, too.

Sally knows that research can continue 24/7. Her favorite databases are now available via cell phone apps so she can do some of this research during soccer practice. She remembers the trusty JSTOR widget she embedded on Facebook so she can get scholarly articles on the scientific impact of environmental catastrophes. Sally uses cell phone apps to search for local fish restaurants, e-mails (or texts) a few proprietors, and arranges a Skype session with a Gulf restaurateur for a personal, credible statement. Sally knows that she can e-mail or text the library or teacher-librarian for support during each stage.

Sally now can access a variety of opinions—and examine news from a variety of lenses—as she tries to discover truth. Blogs, wikis, tweets, and real-time news are all now at her fingertips. Mashpedia is one real-time source her teacher-librarian introduced to pull together a variety of new information formats with constantly updating feeds. To exploit any real-time search tools, Sally must first determine the best hashtag for searching real-time news stories. Who is tweeting or blogging about the issue? Is BP updating the news? Are people living on the Gulf sharing? What about the U.S. government?

Evaluation

Because Sally is using sources of information such as Wikipedia, blogs, and personal information sources, she will have to triangulate (verify via multiple sources) her gathered information to determine its authority and authenticity. She looks for bias, both stated and hidden. Bias is to be understood and noted, not necessarily avoided. Though finding current information is not a problem, Sally must examine at what point in the story each particular tweet or post or document was written; she also considers why it was written and by whom.

Organization and Synthesis

Sally uses a web-based mind-mapping strategy to help her discover patterns and relationships in her findings. She embeds this mind map in her research wiki to share with her teacher and teacher-librarian along with her progress reflections.

Sally also shares Google docs that she is using to draft her written project and storyboard her video with the others who are involved in her project: her teacher-librarian, her teacher, and the restaurateurs.

Documentation

Sally has the option of using fee-based NoodleTools or a variety of free citation generators for creating her lists of works cited and works consulted. This time around she opts to use the free BibMe, which actually pulls most of each citation from a database and then formats all of her citations. Sally will include live links to her online sources in her final products and knows to cite not just textual materials but also the visual and audio data that she used. With the help of the teacher-librarian, Sally interprets and applies fair use guidelines as she selects what materials she can and will use. She also seeks to use Creative Commons music and images when she can. She plans to assign a Creative Commons license to her own work so that others may remix it under conditions that she can control.

All of these formative steps are visible to Sally's teacher in the wiki she maintains for this major project. No need to submit outlines and drafts; the teacher-librarian helped Sally's teacher set up an index of her students' sites so they both might watch and intervene as students progress. She and the teacher-librarian can interact with Sally to ask her pointed questions and guide her work.

Communication

Sally is proud of what she is learning and excited about the video she currently is storyboarding and soon will be producing. Sally considers publishing her work online in the form of a public service announcement on YouTube, Vimeo, or any of a number of other portals for sharing. The broader audience raises Sally's level of concern about the quality of her work. She recognizes the power that images—photographs, graphics, and charts—can play in helping her get her message across in powerful ways. Sally's teacher-librarian helps her put her video together and upload it to a public video portal.

Sally considers her online academic digital footprint and the impact that her work may have on her college studies and her future career. She asks herself, "Will an extreme point of view hurt my chances of getting a job with a more traditional company?" and "Will others be impressed with my academic and intellectual efforts?" And, perhaps even more important, she asks, "Will it make a difference?"

She also opts to publish her formal paper using one of an array of public digital tools in the "cloud"—Issuu, Docstoc, Lulu, Yudu—that make her work look truly professional and will be available to others long after her school accounts are no longer active. Sally sees that her work in high school is part of a lifelong portfolio necessary for advancing in her career.

Final Grade

A nongraded, practically self-created, assessment tool helps Sally determine her areas of strength (clear writing style, good organization) and areas for development (need to see creative insights into work, consider a more global perspective of problem). Continual peer and teacher assessment during the project is more meaningful and helpful to Sally than a final "grade." Sally considers herself a colearner along with her teacher, her teacher-librarian, and her peers as she experiments and uses powerful and purposeful new tools that seem to appear almost daily.

The Evolution of Information Literacy

What has changed for our Sallies over the course of more than twenty years?

1. Information is so much more accessible and students' choices of sources have grown exponentially. Learners can

construct original research with new survey tools. Depending on the context of the information task, students must consider whether they have the right balance of a growing array of sources in traditional and emerging media.

2. Evaluation of information sources has become more important, more sophisticated, and more subjective. Each of us must develop the ability to triangulate the flood of information and media available to mediate truth.

3. For digital citizens, attribution is still the right thing to do. Careful documentation builds academic integrity and prepares learners for scholarship. Online citation generators make the work a bit less onerous and a lot more collaborative. But documentation has grown in complexity, forcing students, online generators, and style guides to attempt to keep up with continually emerging formats.

4. Intellectual property issues require more sophisticated discussion, as Creative Commons becomes an alternative to copyright and as learners themselves remix media. In a remix culture, student producers must learn about current guidelines for using copyrighted materials from the point of view of the creator, not just the consumer.

5. Learners have new strategies for synthesis. A new array of cloud-based brainstorming, mind-mapping, timelining, and storyboarding tools are available, creating rich opportunities for collaborating and sharing.

6. The library collection is both physical and virtual. In addition to expanding the notion of what books physically look like, libraries collect and lend tools for production. Through dynamic pathfinders and websites, librarians not only lead learners to content but also to web-based tools for telling new stories. A school library's collection also may now include students' work and, by doing so, validates and celebrates students' new knowledge.

7. The read and write web has created a genuine audience for student work. Student communication products reach beyond

the traditional term paper and include media appropriate to and effective for their message. Audience gives students a higher level of concern about the quality of their work and encourages them to have an impact on the greater community of interest. Because communication is the end product of research, librarians guide learners in creating projects that best present their newly constructed knowledge.

8. Today's libraries are not only places to get stuff. They are also places to make stuff and do stuff and share stuff.

9. The web makes research a far more independent effort, but with the use of platforms such as blogs or wikis or Google sites the process now can be transparent and interactive. Teacher-librarians help move the research process online, using strategies that some are calling *knowledge-building centers*.

10. The role of the teacher-librarian has shifted from one who gathers, stores, and indexes resources to that of an educator and collaborator who helps students ethically and effectively filter, evaluate, and use information and then do something with it, ideally to communicate in powerful ways with authentic audiences. The librarian becomes an even more critical player in new learning landscapes where information and communication options continually shift.

Resources

American Library Association. (2010, May 10). Comments to the U.S. Department of Education on the National Education Technology Plan. Retrieved from www.wo.ala.org/district dispatch/wp-content/uploads/2010/05/ALA_NETP.pdf

Eisenberg, M., Berkowitz, R., & Johnson, D. (2010). *Information, communications, and technology (ICT) skills curriculum based on the big6 skills approach to information problem-solving*. Retrieved from www.big6.com/2010/02/03/infolit-experts-merge-k-12-technology-literacy-and-information-literacy-into-one-curriculum/

Johnson, D. (2009, July/August). Libraries for a post-literate society. *Multimedia & Internet @ Schools*. Retrieved from www.doug-johnson.com/dougwri/libraries-for-a-post-literate-society.html

Loertscher, D. (2011). *Knowledge building centers*. Retrieved from http://schoollearningcommons.pbworks.com/Knowledge–Building–Centers

Valenza, J. K. (2009, September 21). *14 ways K–12 librarians can teach social media tech & learning*. Retrieved from www.techlearning.com/editorblogs_ektid23558.aspx

Valenza, J. K. (2010, April). Tag team tech: Evolving the virtual school library, deconstructing the essentials. *eVOYAWeb*. Retrieved from http://techlearning.com/blogs/25886

Valenza, J. K., & Johnson, D. (2009, October 1). Things that keep us up at night. *School Library Journal*, pp. 28–32. Retrieved from www.schoollibraryjournal.com/article/CA6699357.html

CHAPTER 13

Online Tool Suites

Diana Laufenberg
and Mark Wagner

An online tool suite is a collection of web-based applications—such as word processing, spreadsheet, electronic presentation, and calendar tools—that work in concert to provide users with an integrated platform for creating, sharing, and collaborating. By concentrating the efforts of technology to support professionals, classroom teachers, and students on a shared set of online tools, the focus is not on getting the technology to function but rather on learning.

WHY WOULD STUDENTS USE ONLINE TOOL SUITES?

Online tool suites offer students a platform to interact with a number of applications that use a consistent framework, set of processes, and terminology. By streamlining the different applications used, students are able to concentrate on creating high-quality work rather than on how to make the applications function properly.

Without online tool suites, student work often is stored on a machine either at school or at home. In this scenario information has to be transported from one place to the other using flash drives or e-mailing work back and forth. This is neither efficient nor effective over the long term. Online tool suites make the work portable, efficient, and accessible by hosting the work "in the cloud." Files can then be accessed from any computer connected to the Internet.

In addition to the technical advantages, students are equipped to collaborate with other students easily within the online tool suite. For instance, in the case of Google Docs, students can share, collaborate, and publish work with people at the desk next to them or halfway around the world. This ability to share work and receive instant or asynchronous feedback is a large motivator for students to engage in dynamic learning processes.

WHY WOULD TEACHERS USE ONLINE TOOL SUITES?

Teachers are motivated to identify processes that challenge students to create high-quality work products. Online tool suites support the teacher by centralizing information, connections, and work products. The ability to share calendars, assignments, and projects within one umbrella of applications means that students can concentrate on creating and the teacher can concentrate on helping them with their educational goals. Teachers are empowered with tools that allow for observation of the learning process, live and in progress.

For all the same reasons that online tool suites are beneficial for student learning, the integrated applications serve teacher professional pursuits as well. Calendar sharing with departments or grade levels, collaborating on interdisciplinary unit planning, and organizing schoolwide events all serve to improve the efficiency and effectiveness of the noninstructional side of the teaching profession.

WHY WOULD ADMINISTRATORS USE ONLINE TOOL SUITES?

The balance among administrative tasks, instructional approaches, and communication media challenges many school communities. Time is frequently cited as one of the top concerns of teachers and administrators. Online tool suites address the time issue in two key ways. First, the time it takes to train and orient staff to online tool suites often is drastically reduced because the applications all share a consistent set of processes and terminology. Second, streamlining digital communication and collaboration with large groups of people enables increased clarity and efficiency.

From a learning perspective, students and educators will be able to use the applications across classes and thus simultaneously limit the amount of instructional time used to teach the tool and increase the amount of minutes available to think, collaborate, and create.

GOOGLE APPS FOR EDUCATION

One popular online tool suite available to schools for free is Google Apps for Education. Rather than hosting e-mail, calendar, and document-sharing systems on their own servers, schools and districts can take advantage of Google's free offer to host these systems (and much more) for them on Google's servers "in the cloud." These services are entirely separate instances of popular consumer products offered by Google, including Gmail, Google Calendar, Google Docs, and Google Sites. All e-mail addresses and sites use the school or district's domain (rather than www.gmail.com, for instance) and district system administrators can control user accounts, which applications are active for users, and a number of other security settings. Many of the applications in this suite can be powerful tools for educational leaders.

Google Mail for Administrators

One of the core applications of Google Apps for Education is Google Mail, which includes all of the features of Gmail but exists within the school's domain. Gmail is built for people such as educational leaders who receive a potentially overwhelming amount of e-mail. Features such as smart filters, custom labels, and keyboard shortcuts make it easy to manage and organize a large amount of mail. Most important, though, Google Mail excels at archiving and searching your mail so that finding important messages is easy, even when your e-mail isn't organized or managed well. Google Labs Experimental features, such as the forgotten attachment detector and canned responses, also can be invaluable time savers.

Google Calendar for Administrators

Another core application in Google Apps for Education is Google Calendar. This is more than just a way to schedule appointments; it also is a reminder service, an organization tool, and a powerful communication and collaboration system. Educational leaders can share their calendars with coworkers, administrative assistants or office managers can be given editing rights to the calendar, and others might only see free or busy notices. School facilities or resources (such as meeting rooms), maps of events (using Google Maps), and documents containing key information (using Google Docs) all can be attached to an event. Calendars can be visible in Google Mail and can be embedded into other websites; this capability is excellent for creating and sharing school calendars that include items such as due dates, athletic schedules, computer lab sign-ups, and more. With some clever set-up, Google Calendar can even be used to send updates to community members at a public website, via e-mail, or through Twitter and Facebook.

Google Docs for Administrators

Google Docs, another core application in Google Apps for Education, is essentially an online version of a desktop office tools suite. Like Microsoft Office, for instance, it includes the ability to create and edit word processing documents, presentations, and spreadsheets. It also includes a drawing element and the ability to collect data via easy-to-use web-based forms.

Because all of the documents (and software) are housed online, there is no need to be concerned about what computer a document is saved on or what software version is installed. In addition, because everything is all online, it is easy for educational leaders to access their documents from any computer—and to share documents with colleagues, allowing multiple users to edit the same document collaboratively (and simultaneously) and avoiding the need to e-mail different versions back and forth as attachments. Because everything is online, Google also keeps a revision history of every edit made to each document (making it easy to recover lost work, fix mistakes, and hold editors accountable). In addition, publishing a document such as a student handbook as a public web page is easy to do when the work is complete.

The online presentation software has additional features, such as the ability to present directly from the web (with no other software needed) and a sidebar chat for audience members or co-presenters. Naturally the spreadsheets have special web-based features too, such as formulas that will populate cells with Google search results. The killer application, though, for educational leaders, may be the Forms feature, which allows easy creation of Web-based forms that enter submitted data directly into a spreadsheet and can automatically create a visual summary of the results. This is ideal for collecting whatever data you need to make true data-driven decisions and can be the key to creating an efficient paperless office.

Google Sites for Administrators

Google Sites is another core Google Apps for Education service. Google Sites makes it possible for any user to easily create, edit, and maintain a frequently updated multimedia website. These sites are appropriate for use at the district, school, or classroom level or for individual student projects or portfolios. Like Google Docs, each Google Site can be shared with other users, allowing multiple colleagues or students to collaborate on the content. And, being well-integrated with other Google services, Google Sites makes it easy to embed not only images and video but also calendars, documents, maps, slideshows, forms, and much more. A variety of themes and templates make it easy to customize the look and feel of each site—and to scaffold site set-up for students. Sites even include announcement pages that can be used by educational leaders as a blog to reach out to the staff, students, and community.

Other Tools in the Google Apps Suite for Administrators

Google Apps for Education includes several other core applications, a handful of Labs applications, and a staggering number of third-party applications now available (often for free to educational institutions) through the Apps Marketplace. Other core services include Google Talk, Google Video, and Google Groups. Google Talk allows instant messaging within the organization (or around the world) and includes the ability to make web-based audio or video calls. Google Video allows schools to host video online in a sort of "walled garden" version of YouTube, and Google Groups allows the creation of online groups that can be used as e-mail list-servs or discussion forums for students, staff, or fellow educational leaders. Creating groups also makes it easier to share resources within the organization.

New Google applications available through Google Labs include Google Moderator, which educational leaders can use to guide staff or community meetings by allowing others to submit questions or ideas and to vote on submissions. Short Links is another Labs service that allows users to easily shorten long web addresses using a new link in the organization's domain. Google Contacts, an organizationwide contacts management system, also is now in beta.

The Apps Marketplace is a venue for third-party applications that can be seamlessly integrated with Google Apps for Education, allowing a single sign-on solution. If the administrator of the domain activates these applications, they are then available to all users, just as Mail, Docs, Sites, and the other core applications would be if activated. Some of the free applications available in the marketplace today that might be helpful for educational leaders include organizational management tools such as EchoSign electronic signatures, MailChimp for e-mail campaigns, Manymoon for project management, ScheduleOnce for setting meetings across domains, SurveyMonkey for more sophisticated surveys than Google Forms can handle, and TripIt for managing travel. Other creative tools may also be useful to educational leaders, teachers, and students, including Aviary design tools for editing images and audio and Creately for online diagramming and mind mapping. The marketplace is always expanding and additional free applications with clear benefits in an educational organization become available often.

SOME GOOGLE APPS SITES

There are numerous resources that can help you use Google Apps. Here are a few to get you started:

Google Apps: www.google.com/a/

Google Apps for Education: www.google.com/a/edu

Google Apps Education Community: http://edu.googleapps .com/

Google Apps Education Training Center: http://edutraining .googleapps.com/

Google Apps Marketplace: www.google.com/enterprise/
marketplace/

Google Apps Marketplace EDU Specialists: http://goo.gl/Zl5q

SUMMARY

Although this chapter focused on Google Apps for Education to
illustrate the viability of online tool suites, similar services are
available from Zoho, Microsoft, and other providers. Research
various tools carefully to determine which is best for you and your
school organization.

In many cases, the technical set-up for an online tool suite,
such as Google Apps for Education, takes only a matter of minutes, although integration with existing systems, such as Microsoft's
Active Directory, may require additional synchronization. The
most important decisions will not be technical. Reading about and
visiting schools that have already made the switch can provide
valuable experience and guidance. A pilot group of users (representing students, teachers, administrators, and support staff) also
may be invaluable in determining how best to configure the suite
and to identify what policies (and professional development) are
necessary for the tools to be used to their fullest potential.

Resources

CUE, Inc., & WestEd. (2010a). *Gmail in the classroom*. Google
Teacher Academy Resources. Retrieved from http://goo
.gl/myl6r

CUE, Inc., & WestEd. (2010b). *Google calendar in the
classroom*. Google Teacher Academy Resources. Retrieved from
http://goo.gl/gET3u

CUE, Inc., & WestEd. (2010c). *Google docs in the classroom*. Google
Teacher Academy Resources. Retrieved from http://goo
.gl/4pba

CUE, Inc., & WestEd. (2010d). *Google sites in the classroom.* Google Teacher Academy Resources. Retrieved from http://goo.gl/vz3uo

Pavicich, C., & CUE, Inc. (2010). *More apps for your domain.* Google Teacher Academy Resources. Retrieved from http://goo.gl/mVa31

Role, S., & CUE, Inc. (2010). *Google docs for administrators.* Google Teacher Academy Resources. Retrieved from http://goo.gl/rt9Wt

Silva, D., & CUE, Inc. (2010). *Google calendar for administrators.* Google Teacher Academy Resources. Retrieved from http://goo.gl/pGHuh

Thiele, H., & CUE, Inc. (2010). *Administration, control panel, and postini.* Google Teacher Academy Resources. Retrieved from http://goo.gl/mVa31

Thiele, H., Pavicich, C., & CUE, Inc. (2010). *Gmail for administrators.* Google Teacher Academy Resources. Retrieved from http://goo.gl/RuIuF

Thumann, L., & CUE, Inc. (2010). *Google sites for administrators.* Google Teacher Academy Resources. Retrieved from http://goo.gl/mVa31

CHAPTER 14

Twitter

Alec Couros

and Kevin Jarrett

According to a recent study, 19 percent of all Internet users use Twitter or another social networking service (SNS) to send and receive information about themselves and others they care about (Fox, Zickuhr, & Smith, 2009). Less than a year earlier, that figure was 11 percent. This increase of 72 percent in less than a year represents a challenge and an opportunity for innovative school leaders and districts. Here's why: according to the same Pew Research Center study, the individuals most likely to use Twitter or another SNS are Internet users ages eighteen to forty-four, representing two key stakeholder groups important to every school leader. The first: parents in their childbearing years; the second: teachers and staff in the district (National Center for Education Statistics, 2004). The question, therefore, is what implications does Twitter have for you and your school community?

THE POWER OF TWITTER

Wikipedia defines Twitter as "a social networking and microblogging service that enables its users to send and read other user messages called tweets" (http://en.wikipedia.org/wiki/Twitter). Tweets are text-based messages of up to 140 characters that can be sent and received from computers and mobile devices connected to the Internet. Although Twitter has grown into a global phenomenon for its social and casual communication value, increasing numbers of professionals—including educators, administrators, school districts, and community groups—are using Twitter as a means of sharing information and building school communities. A spreadsheet (http://bit.ly/dbtXay) created by Palm Beach County, Florida, teacher Lee Kolbert tracks almost one hundred school districts' use of Twitter in the classroom and as a district communication tool. A blog posting at Online Universities, *100 Inspiring Ways to Use Social Media in the Classroom* (http://bit.ly/cAhLCf) provides several rich examples of Twitter's use in K–12 classrooms. As the post points out, creative teachers everywhere use Twitter's free global network to facilitate communication between classrooms, bring outside experts into lesson conversations, and provide updates on school happenings to interested parents and community members. Twitter's instantaneous yet asynchronous nature—tweets are transmitted instantaneously but are stored online in the stream of those following the user— makes it ideal for collaborations and communications, whether they are across the hall, across town, or across the globe.

CAVEATS

Twitter's open nature does present some challenges to districts seeking to use the tool for institutional purposes. By default, tweets are public, meaning that anyone with Internet access can read them at any time. Tweets can be "protected" (made private), thus giving the owner of the Twitter account the ability to approve each recipient (called a "follower") who then can see all the tweets sent (the "stream" or "timeline"). School leaders, especially those in larger districts, should weigh the decision to protect employees' Twitter streams against the administrative effort required to do so; managing a large and growing protected Twitter account (vetting and approving followers, blocking inappropriate ones, and so on) can be tedious. In classroom settings, however, protected Twitter accounts are easily managed by classroom teachers.

LOOKING BEYOND THE LIMITATIONS

These caveats aside, there are substantial potential benefits to embracing Twitter in school settings for everything from instructional support to professional development to administrative communications. In the classroom, teachers can use protected Twitter accounts to communicate with other groups of learners either instantaneously or asynchronously. Private Twitter accounts could be created for individual students as early as elementary school, allowing them to participate in Twitter conversations directly, providing these students with an authentic global audience with whom to share ideas, ask questions, and get information otherwise not available on the public Internet. From a professional development perspective, Twitter affords educators the opportunity to create a personal learning network, essentially a collection of like-minded professionals with common interests who use Twitter to trade information, share resources, ask and answer questions, and debate and discuss educational issues of the day. The benefits of these networks can be enormous as educators are able to assemble a collection of literally "the best and the brightest" practitioners from around the world, individuals with whom the average teacher usually would never have the chance to interact with or learn from. Twitter also can facilitate communication with parents and the school community overall, including updates on events such as class projects, school events, sports scores, awards, breaking news, and even school closure information.

GETTING STARTED

Those involved in the implementation of a technology such as Twitter in a school district setting should first become strongly familiar with the tool through personal and professional use.

Twitter is unlike many other tools in that it relies heavily on social connections to be of any value. Although the technology itself is quite simple, the more crucial understandings lie in the intricacies of social interactions of Twitter users: the sharing of resources, the act of asking questions, and the conversations that ensue. It is only through time and immersion in the tool and social network that this understanding will be achieved.

Here are some steps to get you on your way:

1. Sign up for an account at http://twitter.com.

2. Choose a user name that is as brief as possible and that relates well to your identity. Your user name will be a part of all your tweets and those who reply to you or retweet you, so economy of characters and recognizability are favorable traits.

3. Upload a profile image that is appropriate to your identity and that you are comfortable using for a longer term. As people become connected to others on Twitter, the profile image becomes an important point of reference and often an inseparable part of your digital identity.

4. Complete your profile. Doing so will allow others to know a bit about who you are and the interactions and connections that you seek. This bit of text is crucial information for pro-spective followers.

5. Follow other active Twitter users. You can do this individu-ally if you know an individual's Twitter user name or you can autofollow an entire recommended group by using individuals' Twitter lists or a TweepML list focused on educational admin-istrators (for example, tweepml.org/?t=1602). The Twitter for Teachers wiki (twitter4teachers.pbworks.com) is another good source of Twitter users to follow.

6. Observe interactions. Many new users often are hesitant to jump right in with their first tweet. Sometimes a period

of study and observation is useful to get a sense of the type and breadth of interactions that are common in Twitter communities.

7. Get introduced. Chances are that you may know an educator who is already involved in a Twitter community. Although not necessary, having another user introduce you to members of their personal learning network will increase the chance that you will gain followers and may provide some personal and professional context.

8. Jump in. Ask questions. Share resources. Join in conversations. Follow other intriguing individuals listed in tweets. Twitter communities are very helpful and forgiving, especially to new participants. In a short period of time, you will be on your way to using Twitter as a powerful professional networking tool and you will have insight into further implementation of the tool within your district.

SUMMARY

Districts need to be sure that applicable policies and codes of conduct are updated to encompass text-based communication tools such as Twitter (without mentioning it per se because new tools are always emerging). Staff need to be fully aware of protocols and expectations surrounding communications via these new channels. The explosion of electronic communication devices and services such as Twitter is more proof that districts need to develop and communicate social media policies that afford district staff the flexibility to use these new tools while protecting the district from possible litigation.

References

Fox, S., Zickuhr, K., & Smith, A. (2009, October 21). *RT: More Americans tweeting*. Pew Research Center Publications.

Retrieved from http://pewresearch.org/pubs/1385/who-uses-twitter-tweets

National Center for Education Statistics. (2004). *Schools and staffing survey (SASS)*. Retrieved from http://nces.ed.gov/surveys/sass

CHAPTER 15

Online Images and Visual Literacy

Kimberly Cofino

and David Jakes

With the explosion of mobile phones and their associated cameras—coupled with a wide variety of social media tools—anyone with a phone can be a photographer with the ability to distribute images worldwide with a few clicks. Similarly, ordinary citizens' access to graphic design tools formerly only available to professionals has resulted in an outpouring of images on the web. Flickr, one of the earliest photo-sharing websites, now boasts almost five billion images, with five to six thousand images added every minute by photographers across the globe. However, even Flickr pales in comparison to Facebook, the world's largest social media platform, which receives over sixty million photograph uploads per week and serves one hundred thousand images back to users per second (Beaver, 2007).

A THREEFOLD CHALLENGE

Now that enormous numbers of photographs and images are finding their way online, schools and learners are presented with challenges and opportunities. As can be expected with such large volumes of photography so readily accessible, students may occasionally encounter some inappropriate images. But conversely, image-sharing sites such as Flickr are filled with world-class photography that can be used in new ways by students to create products of value that demonstrate understanding in a process known as *remixing*. The challenge to schools is threefold:

- Provide the necessary technical infrastructure and policy to support the use of Internet images in schools.

- Set appropriate expectations for students while searching online for images.

- Provide professional development for teachers on the use of online images to support student learning.

To meet this challenge in a way that supports learning, schools must help students understand how to be ethical digital citizens. This can be accomplished in part by providing teachers and students opportunities to explore media that supports Creative Commons (http:// creativecommons.org) licensing. A Creative Commons licensing system enables each content creator to apply a license to his or her work that specifies how others may use it, with the specific intent of *encouraging* use and remixing. What is especially exciting about this licensing system is that students and teachers now can use the intellectual property of others legally in their own projects. Such Creative Commons license designations as "attribution only" indicate to individuals that they may use media with this license in any way they desire as long as the original creator receives attribution (citation) in the derivative product. Being able to actually source the original creator of the work helps students understand the importance of proper citation while at the same time facilitating their understanding of ethical use of online intellectual property.

Another unique facet of Creative Commons licensing is that it encourages individuals to share their intellectual property and their passions with a wider audience. By understanding and applying Creative Commons licensing to their own work, students can participate and contribute to online communities that support and extend their learning while at the same time enabling them to explore their personal creative interests. By being able to legally share and license their work, students are becoming legitimate authors, photographers, and videographers. It is empowering for students to see their intellectual property be used by another and recognized for its creative merit.

In short, Creative Commons allows teachers and students to better understand the concept of intellectual property ownership in the digital age, to honor and respect content creators' rights, and to use that content ethically and legally in their own works.

VISUAL MEDIA AND LITERACY

The massive amount of images and other visual media that we are exposed to and have access to suggests a new skill set, one that contributes to shifting notions of literacy. Traditionally, we think of literacy as the ability to read and write. However, understanding how to decode images, how to navigate multimedia, and how to create in these formats has expanded our interpretation of what it means to be literate. In a world dominated by the Internet, always-on advertising, YouTube videos, on-demand movies, video games, and even television, it is critical that students are capable of processing media and have the ability to locate, manage, interpret, and use images to communicate ideas and passions.

The extensive availability of photos and images shared online provides a wide range of opportunities for teachers to help students build visual literacy skills. Such skills including reading pictures as you would read words in a story and developing meaning from those images by themselves, together in a sequence, or hyperlinked throughout a network. Regular experiences in analyzing or decoding images, from basic to the complex, can be easily integrated into classroom practice by providing students with a simple interpretive writing prompt. Teachers can find unique Creative Commons images using Flickr's "interesting" button (which sorts images by the amount of times they are chosen as "favorites" by users) and then ask students to write an interpretive story based on their evaluation of the images.

Another critical aspect of decoding images is analysis of the information found in advertisements as well as visual representations such as charts, maps, and graphs. Determining which medium is best for a specific purpose or communicating complex data in a simple graphic are examples of critical skills for today's students. Being able to distinguish advertisements from editorial content and efficiently grasping the use of navigation structures such as menus and buttons to find, sort, and store needed information or media also are components involved in visual literacy proficiency. Incorporating data-display projects that require students to conduct independent research and then present the results using Excel, Numbers, or other graphing software would be an effective way to integrate these skills into curriculum expectations.

Along with being able to analyze and decode images, students also need experience in creating media-rich works to demonstrate their level of visual literacy. Using tools such as PowerPoint, Keynote, iMovie, or PhotoStory to tell a digital story gives students the opportunity to create media and craft a message of personal importance. These products can be presented to classmates or can be distributed across the networks of the Internet to a worldwide audience.

SUMMARY

As it becomes easier to contribute to and access media on the Internet, and as we continue to rely more and more on multimedia messages to convey ideas and meaning, the ability to navigate a media-rich world becomes increasingly important. Learning institutions should consciously and creatively explore instructional methodologies and learning environments that promote the development of visual literacy skills to ensure that students can effectively navigate the twenty-first-century media landscape.

Reference

Beaver, D. (2007, May 21). Facebook photos infrastructure. *The Facebook blog*. Retrieved from http://blog.facebook.com/blog.php?post=2406207130

CHAPTER 16

Mobile Phones and Mobile Learning

Liz Kolb and Sharon Tonner

The term *mobile phone* brings with it connotations of a handheld device that transmits or receives calls or texts. Many educators still view mobile phones in this manner, possibly due to their own limited usage of their devices. The reality is that many mobile phones now are smart phones—powerful computers that fit nicely in the palm of one's hand. Many of today's mobile devices have touch screens, GPS navigation, digital media playback, camera, video, Internet browsing, the ability to download thousands of applications, and, more recently, video conferencing. These powerful devices enable not just communication but also personalization, collaboration, creativity, and innovation via the consumption, creation, and sharing of content. They remove the restrictions of location-based retrieving and sharing of information and enable anytime, anyplace, anywhere engagement.

WHAT IS MOBILE LEARNING?

Mobile learning, or m-learning, is viewed by some as an extension of electronic learning (or e-learning) that occurs using a handheld device that can be easily transported to different locations (Smith, 2008). Geography is now less of an issue as mobile learning enables the user to access information, interact with materials, create and share learning, and communicate with others without, to a certain extent, being location dependent. Today's mobile phones are no longer just talking and texting devices but "sleek digital Swiss army knives" (Tapscott, 2008, p. 48) with arrays of powerful tools. Users' mobiles become individualized learning and storage devices that are customized to their requirements, whether this be access to personalized learning materials or simple adaptation of the devices for voice recognition, font size, and so on. Mobile phones provide platforms that are adaptable to different learning needs and styles.

M-learning also enables instant access to information and collaboration with others. This instant communication, content retrieval, and sharing is part of today's digital culture and goes against the traditional model of educational institutes as the gate-keepers of information (Traxler, 2008). Mobile learning devices enable users to access learning material as and when they wish in order to extend and deepen their knowledge.

WHY EMBED MOBILE PHONES INTO EDUCATION?

The evidence to support embedding mobile phones into teaching and learning is beginning to emerge through various research reports. One of the key reasons for adopting mobile phones into the learning environment is due to their overwhelming presence in teachers' and learners' lives. For example, a study of mobile phone usage of American teenagers showed that mobile phone ownership rose from 45 percent in 2004 to 75 percent in 2009, with a staggering average of 3,145 text messages sent and received each month (Lenhart, Ling, Campbell, & Purcell, 2009). The work of Tapscott and Williams (2006) and others reinforces that mobile phones provide hubs of connectivity to peers.

This constant connectivity, which is the main reason that youth between twelve and fifteen claim they have a mobile (Ofcom, 2006), is a capacity that can be tapped into in education. Mobile technology is dramatically changing how we communicate, share content, and retrieve information, especially for a generation of youth who are used to the immediate and collaborative nature of the informal learning they engage in outside the constraints of their formalized learning in schools. At school, youth have to dis-connect from the hub of activity in the palm of their hands and try to connect to a didactic style of learning; this is difficult for many. Educators need to look at the potential of these powerful devices and embrace the new learning opportunities that they afford. The focus should be on enabling children to use the tools of their time rather than simply the tools of their teachers.

At the university level, a study of student mobile phone usage (Wang, Shen, Novak, & Pan, 2009) found that m-learning did the following:

- Encouraged and supported anytime, anyplace learning
- Made learning more convenient and accessible to learners' needs
- Made learning more engaging
- Enabled collaborative learning and knowledge construction using contemporary synchronous and asynchronous tools
- Provided a means of formative assessment
- Enabled all students to be active in the learning process

Barriers, Risks, and Precautions Associated with Mobile Learning

Although there are many positive educational benefits to embed-ding mobile devices into the learning environment, these benefits come with new behaviors that require appropriate precautions to be put in place prior to successful integration. These precautions include the development of rules and structures for appropriate use rather than simply waiting for students to use mobile phones inappropriately in the learning setting and then punishing them. Teachers are aware that students can and do use mobile phones in distracting and destructive ways such as cheating, sexting, or secretly taking and posting photos and videos of teachers or other students. Mobile phones are seen by most teachers as a disruptive influence on learning in the classroom due to students texting messages under the desk while the teacher is talking to the class (Evans, 2010). This is no different from students writing notes to one another during a lesson and passing them to their peers; the behavior, not the technology, is the underlying problem. Educators should focus on behavioral concerns, not specific technologies (which constantly change). For example, students who use their mobile phones to take pictures of tests and send them to friends are cheating. It is the act of cheating that should be confronted, not the particular tool used. Teachers should enforce school con-sequences for cheating and make sure that students and educators address why there is a felt need to cheat. If educators just take away the tool, students can always just find another way to cheat. Rather than ban the devices that young people use daily outside the edu-cational setting, school leaders can create rules and structures for successful, safe, and appropriate integration of mobile devices into the learning environment.

PREPARING TO IMPLEMENT MOBILE TECHNOLOGIES

Whether schools choose to provide smart phones to students or have students use their own mobile phones, students still must be well prepared to use the devices in their learning environ-ment. Although school provision of smart phones helps ease some concerns, it does not keep students 100 percent safe or secure from inappropriate uses. Therefore, some boundaries and structures need to be in place *before* students use their mobile phones for classroom learning purposes. Following are some brief guidelines for mobile phone integration in schools.

Addressing Mobile Safety and Appropriate Use

Before teachers implement mobile phones in learning, they must educate students on safety and appropriate uses of mobile phones inside and outside of the classroom. It is important that students understand the consequences of sending pictures, videos, text messages, and making phone calls. Following are three issues that should be addressed as part of a mobile safety lesson:

- *Digital footprints.* Students need to understand that everything they do on a mobile phone can be traced back to them (even years later). This could affect the students' future relationships or employment.
- *Public record.* All information on mobile phones (even some deleted information) is stored by the phone's provider. Therefore every text message, picture message, phone call, or video can be traced back to the student and possibly used against them in a court of law.
- *Sexting, bullying, and other inappropriate uses.* Students need to understand the school disciplinary, legal, personal, and other consequences of using mobile phones inappropriately.

If schools are providing smart phones to students, they may consider loading mobile spy software (for example, www.mobile-spy.com) onto the phones in order to track students' activities on each device.

Students' Personal Devices

When mobile phones belong to students rather than the school, educators have far less control over what is on the phones, how the phones work, and what students can do with the devices.

As a result, some schools prefer to relegate mobile phone use to assignments that occur outside of the school environment, such as for homework or field trips. Other schools are modifying their policies to generally allow for student mobile phone usage on campus for learning but also accommodate individual instructors' wishes regarding restriction (see, for example, Ruan & Chambers, 2008). Here are some examples of what many schools include in their modifed policies:

- Students should have mobile phones on silent mode when not being used for instruction.

- The use of communication features on cellular devices during instructional time or in a disruptive manner in the school atmosphere is prohibited.

- Each teacher has the right to allow the use of mobile devices (for example, mobile phones, laptops, iPods, personal data assistants) during instructional time.

- Each teacher can decide on a location in the classroom where they would like students to place their mobile devices when not being used for instruction.

- The use of mobile phones in the hallway is prohibited because it is considered a disruption to classes taking place.

- Nondisruptive mobile phone use is allowed in the stairwells.

- Students are permitted to use mobile devices, including mobile phones, in the student lounge.

- Consequences for using mobile phones to cheat or disrupt class will be the same as the consequences for cheating and school disruption in the school's regular policy.

As mentioned previously, it is much easier for schools to control mobile devices when they provide them for students. In these instances, school districts often will turn off the texting or telephone features of the smart phones. This allows students to use the smart phones' mobile Internet and Bluetooth features but enables finer control over use of the devices for personal communications.

Involving Students

Once students have been educated about mobile safety and the school has decided on a general mobile device policy, individual teachers often will work with students to come up with additional rules and regulations they deem appropriate for mobile phone use in the classroom. Students who are engaged in the rule-making process feel greater ownership over the rules and tend to follow them more readily. Some examples of classroom-level rules include the following:

- Mobile phones should be off or on vibrate when not being used.

- Mobile phones should be on students' desks (face down) or at the front of the room on the teacher's desk when not being used in class.

- No media should be sent from one mobile phone to another (or to the Internet) that is unrelated to class during class time.

- No media that contains information, images, or representations of another individual in class should be sent to another phone or posted online without explicit permission from the individual whom it is about.

Once safety concerns, school regulations, and classroom rules have been addressed, educators should survey their students to find out what they can do on their mobile devices without incurring overcharges. This is only necessary if students are using their own mobile phones rather than school-provided smart phones. The survey results allow educators to understand the activities that they can do most often with the students' devices. For example, if a teacher knows that most of her students have unlimited text messaging, the teacher can elect to do more texting activities for learning either inside or outside of the classroom.

Involving Parents

It is vital that parents are informed about mobile phone usage to foster classroom learning. In order to inform parents, educators can engage in a variety of activities, including the following:

- Send home a detailed permission form about mobile phone activity
- During parent night or an open house, address the mobile phone activity
- Hold a special workshop for parents to teach them about mobile safety and how to model appropriate use with their own children (to reinforce and extend what the students are learning in the classroom)

The following guidelines might be given to parents to help them assist their children with mobile phone safety and usage.

Model Appropriate Use

Never talk on the phone or text while driving. Try not to interrupt conversations or dinners with mobile phone activities. Also explain and point out to the children when you are modeling an appropriate use such as, "I am not answering the phone because we are having a family dinner and I want to give my full attention to my family for this hour."

Document Family Activities

Model how to capture pictures or videos of family vacations or family activities via the mobile phone. Demonstrate how to capture reactions (via audio recording) to family activities. This is a great way to model data collection in the real world.

Learn More

Visit websites (for example, http://connectsafely.com) that have ideas on how to stay safe while using mobile phones.

Get Involved with Classroom Projects

Because parents often have their mobile phones with them all day, they could capture images or send text messages into class for the school assignment along with their children. They could join the class text message alert system in order to receive information from the teacher about homework or other class activities.

Innovative Examples of How to Embed Mobile Phones into the Learning Environment

Mobile phones allow teachers to meet many of their instructional needs. For example teachers can use mobile phones to individualize learning, to extend learning beyond the school day, to get students involved in the greater community, to engage or motivate students in the classroom curricula, to save classroom teaching time, to help students engage in literacy learning, to improve the home-to-school connection, and to allow students immediate access to information and research. Following are a few examples of how teachers are meeting some of these learning goals.

Student-Centered Learning

Mobile phones (especially smart phones) can allow opportunities for an individualized curriculum that is personalized to a student's needs. Different learning styles can be catered to using quick response (QR) codes to provide a more multimedia learning experience. QR codes are essentially bar codes for mobile phones. A student who takes a picture of a QR code with a mobile phone immediately receives information on the phone pertaining to that code. The student needs to have downloaded free QR code or bar code reader software onto the phone in order to read QR codes.

Examples of using QR codes to personalize learning include embedding them in workbooks to support or extend a child's learning, personalizing outdoor learning, engaging children with classroom displays through codes of various colors that relate to different learning groups, and using them to formatively assess students.

Extending Learning

Mobile phones can be used for homework, on field trips, or during school breaks to extend learning outside of the classroom setting. Here are some examples:

- Students and parents can sign up for an optional text message of the day around a particular curricular topic. This could be done using a text alert (see, for example, Tell My Cell at www.tellmycell.com).

- During a field trip, students can use the audio and camera functions on their phones and send their files to a secure website (see, for example, ipadio at www.ipadio.com) that can be accessed when students return to school.

- Many mobile devices have GPS capabilities, which allow students to track locations. Students can use a website such as GPS Mission (www.gpsmission.com) for outdoor learning or to become familiar with a new environment.

- Students can use a mapping site (see, for example, MapMyRUN at www.mapmyrun.com) in physical education to keep track of their time and distance for bikes, hikes, and runs.

- Students could develop mapping skills by taking mobile pictures outside of school and then tagging the pictures using the location-based aspect of phones and viewing them on sites such as Flickr (www.flickr.com) or Flagr (www.flagr.com).

Classroom Engagement

Using mobile phones in learning also can create opportunities for enhanced student engagement. One example might be a teacher's use of a web-based polling resource such as Poll Everywhere (www .polleverywhere.com), which can be used with mobile phone text messaging. A teacher could quickly set up a text message poll for the students to take during class. One of the benefits of text message polling is that it can be anonymous, so students who usually are a bit afraid to express their ideas because of social pressures can freely give their opinions without fear of ridicule. In addition, these types of sites often allow for anonymous brainstorming. Instead of a multiple choice poll, the teacher could ask the students to text message open-ended responses to a polling site.

Literacy Interaction

English students often struggle with understanding classic English poetry and literature. By using new literacies (such as text messaging) with which the students are familiar, teachers can help students make connections to more difficult English writings. Here are some examples:

- PK–2 students who are working on early literacy can download literacy learning tools from PBS (www.pbskids.org) to their mobile phones.
- Older students can write their own text messaging novels (see, for example, Textnovel at www.textnovel.com), selecting specific genres on which to focus.
- Students can create their own digital storybooks or clay animations on a smart phone by using the mobile pictures or video on their phones and then editing on the mobile Internet using tools such as JayCut (www.jaycut.com).

There are many other opportunities as well. For example, English teachers often worry that their students do not understand how to summarize classic English writing. When they ask students to summarize a scene from Shakespeare's *Romeo and Juliet*, for instance, students may just transcribe word-for-word from classic to modern-day English instead of giving an overview of the scene. However, if asked to summarize the scene via text message(s), students would have to put more thought into what happened and identify the most significant actions from the scene. Students would be forced to move beyond a simple transcription of the novel and consider all of the interactions happening in the literature.

Instant Access to Information

Students no longer need to be in the library or even at a computer in order to access quality information and conduct research. Using their mobile devices, students can access, research, and store information on the go. Here are some examples:

- Students can send a text query and receive information (see, for example, ChaCha at www.chacha.com or DOTGO at www.dotgo.com).

- Students can make a phone call and listen to any podcast or web page (see, for example, Dial2Do at www.dial2do.com or Podlinez at www.podlinez.com).

- Students can download books to their smart phones.

- Students can use their mobile devices to make notes and access those notes on the go (see, for example, Evernote at www.evernote.com).

- School librarians can set up text message alert systems that enable students to send in a text query and receive an answer (see, for example, Tell My Cell at www.tellmycell .com).

SUMMARY

In today's world, where learning is no longer confined to educational environments using the tools and methods of the past, using mobile phones in the learning environment enables children to access the tools of their generation rather than just those of their predecessors. Mobile phones enable children to communicate, collaborate, create, co-create, and share their learning with their peers and a wider audience. The restrictions that formerly confined learning to a centralized location are now removed to enable learning to take place anytime, anyplace, anywhere. As we think about mobile phones in education, we should reflect on the words of Ignacio Estrada: "If children don't learn the way we teach, maybe we should teach the way they learn."

References

Evans, J. (2010). *Mobile devices + Web 2.0 = Engaged and empowered learners.* Presentation given at the International Society and Technology in Education Annual Conference, Denver, Colorado.

Lenhart, A., Ling, R., Campbell, S., & Purcell, K. (2010). *Teens and mobile phones.* Retrieved from www.pewinternet.org/Reports/2010/Teens-and-Mobile-Phones.aspx

Ofcom. (2006, May 2). *Media literacy audit. Report on media literacy amongst children.* Retrieved from http://stakeholders.ofcom.org.uk/binaries/research/media-literacy/children.pdf

Ruan, G., & Chambers, I. (2008). *Can you hear us now? New mobile phone policy on the way.* Retrieved from www.uni.illinois.edu//og/news/2008/10/can-you-hear-us-now-cell-phone-policy

Smith, R. (2008). *GoMobile! Maximising the potential of mobile technologies for learners with disabilities.* London: Learning Skills Network.

Tapscott, D. (2008). *Grown up digital: How the net generation is changing your world.* New York: McGraw-Hill.

Tapscott, D., & Williams, A. D. (2006). *Wikinomics: How mass collaboration changes everything.* London: Atlantic Books.

Traxler, J. (2008). *Modernity, mobility and the digital divides.* Retrieved from http://repository.alt.ac.uk/442

Wang, M., Shen, R., Novak, D., & Pan, X. (2009). The impact of mobile learning on students' learning behaviours and performance: Report from a large blended classroom. *British Journal of Educational Technology,* 40(4), 673–695.

Additional Resources

Attewell, J., Savill-Smith, C., & Douch, R. (2009). *The impact of mobile learning: Examining what it means for teaching and learning.* London: LSN.

Berkman Center for Internet & Society. (2008). *Digital dossier.* Retrieved from www.youtube.com/watch?v=79IYZVYIVLA

Gavin, J. (2008). *U.K. PC & mobile Internet usage report.* London: Comscore.

International Telecommunication Union. (2010). *World telecommunication/ICT development report 2010: Monitoring the WSIS targets. A mid-term review.* Geneva: Author.

Kennedy, T., Smith, A., Wells, A. T., & Wellman, B. (2008). *Networked families.* Pew Internet & American Life Project. Retrieved from www.pewinternet.org/Reports/2008/Networked-Families.aspx

CHAPTER 17

Social Networking

Ewan McIntosh

and Jeff Utecht

If you're a commercial technology start-up with a bright idea, a video game company looking for new players, or a brand trying to engage with eight- to eighteen-year-olds, social networks are where you spend your time, energy, and vast sums of money. Schools have, by and large, resisted the siren call of social network culture to engage learners in new ways and on new planes. But why is this the case?

A social network is a website that brings people together by sharing their news, photographs, videos, and events. When you visit or log on to a social network, you are greeted with a different, updated version of the latest news from your contacts. Social network creators design their networks primarily to encourage existing members to sign up their friends, family, and contacts. As schools seek more and better ways to connect with their local communities, the ingredients of social networks present an attractive means to do so.

THE UBIQUITY OF SOCIAL NETWORKS

Facebook is currently the social network du jour for North American, European, Singaporean, and Chilean populations (*Countries with top Facebook penetration to population*, 2010): it's a youth center, shopping mall, and video game arcade for over half a billion of the world's seven billion souls. It's the United States' second-most popular video site after YouTube (Lardinois, 2010). In the United Kingdom (UK), using a social network is more popular than using a search engine (*Social networks now more popular than search engines in the UK*, 2010).

Social networking outside North America and Europe is booming even more. Orkut, Google's social network based in Brazil, dominates South America with over one hundred million members (Wikipedia, 2011), and Chinese social networks collectively outpace Facebook, MySpace, and Orkut altogether. The top three social networks there (QQ, 51.cn, and Baidu) pool around 616 million members, and Chinese social networks generate more use—and revenues from advertising for their creators—than any others (Godula, Li, & Yu, 2009). Most of these users are not under eighteen. The population of thirty-five- to fifty-four-year-olds constitutes Facebook's largest demographic (*Older users becoming dominant on Facebook*, n.d.).

Their widespread use makes social networks a compelling platform through which to engage school communities: if not youngsters themselves, certainly their parents and wider families. What school system does not seek to engage more with these groups? In Glasgow, Scotland, for example, one in five parents said they would like to use Facebook as a more handy, regular means of checking in to see what their child is learning and how their child is doing (Churchill, 2010).

EDUCATIONAL USES
OF SOCIAL NETWORKING TOOLS

Gunn Elementary School in Omaha, Nebraska, has used Facebook to engage parents in the learning of first-graders (scho, n.d.). Status updates regularly reveal what has been learned in class that day and the process of condensing learning into short updates is an ideal synthesis activity for learners. Event invitations sent via Facebook mean that parents have less chance of missing out on a letter sent home. Notes allow teachers and management to share longer, more formal news with parents, and private messages allow the school to interact directly with a parent without having to request hundreds of e-mail addresses at the start of the year. Videos and photographs of student work can be shared in a click.

During the November 2010 midterm elections in the United States, many school districts found it hard to get information out to voters about levy and bond issues. What Facebook has done is change the culture of where we go to be updated on what is happening in our community. Instead of spending time looking for information, voters were spending their time on Facebook. The Fairfax County Virginia public school system is one district that has captured the use of Facebook with their community. The district's Facebook page (www.facebook.com/fcpsva) has over fifteen thousand subscribers. Every time the district publishes an update to its Facebook page, those fifteen thousand people receive the information in their Facebook news stream. Instead of posting information on the district website and making people come to them, they take the content to the community.

Facebook is compelling for one reason in particular: meeting parents, caregivers, and learners in the space where they "hang out" already. None of these groups have to make an effort to sign up to a new social network (a disadvantage of creating "new" social networks on platforms such as Ning or on your school's virtual learning environment), yet they can "accidentally" bump into content and interact with the school on a far more regular basis than they currently do. An additional reason Facebook is appealing for those schools with tight budgets is the fact that Facebook is free to use.

But schools needn't always opt for a space like Facebook. Schools can and do create freestanding, social networklike environments around learning.

SOCIAL NETWORKLIKE
SYSTEMS BUILT AROUND BLOGS

Some of the most pioneering work in understanding the wider potential of social media has been done in the school district of East Lothian, Scotland. Since 2003 students, teachers, and parents have used blogs to share the learning going on inside classrooms with the wider world. In 2006 all of these were brought under one, memorable web address (http://eduBuzz.org) on a WordPress multiuser platform, and in 2008 a social networklike homepage (with the BuddyPress plug-in) was introduced that shows the latest comments and uploads from the whole network. Every day visitors arrive on the home page and are faced with yet more marvels of learning from across the district's forty-five schools and headquarters. Around three hundred thousand unique visitors every month see what is going on in East Lothian schools, and teachers and parents alike report feeling much more connected to each other and to what learning looks like in each classroom.

At the International School Bangkok in Bangkok, Thailand, every fourth- through twelfth-grader is given full control over a blog that is open to the Internet (http://blogs.isb.ac.th). Through this platform, teachers can teach students how to be safe on the web and at the same time teach them how to create a positive profile or digital footprint. The school is starting to use the blogs as an e-portfolio system by having students categorize some of their best reflections. Because students are reflecting on their life in and out of school, teachers get a better view of the whole by reading blog posts from other classes or about the students' life outside of school.

PROTECTING THE IMAGE
OF YOUR LEARNING INSTITUTION

When it comes to creating and protecting your school's image on the web, it's vital to understand where your audience—parents, community leaders, potential students—choose to spend time online. If they are on Facebook, for example, then you need to know how your school is represented there. In recent years there has been an expectation that a school's brochure-ware website was sufficient to project a positive image of learning at the school. Before that, school leaders might worry about what the message board at the school gates said or about making sure that when community members drove by, the playground was clean, paint wasn't peeling, and everything was ready for students. We're used to cleaning, pruning, and just occasionally curating a physical image of our schools that we project out to the community. In today's socially networked world, not only do principals and leaders need to be aware of what the physical image of their school portrays but also what is portrayed by the digital image of their school—and people's reactions to it.

TRY THIS

Take some time right now to open up your computer and search for your school in a variety of social networking spaces. As you do so, ask yourself, "If I were a community member, parent, or student, what message am I getting?"

1. Start at YouTube. At the top there is a search bar. Type in the name of your school and take some time to watch and skim through the results. How is your school portrayed on YouTube?

2. Next go to Facebook. If you have an account, log in and search for groups with your school name (if you don't have an account, create one). How is your school portrayed on Facebook?

3. Next head to Google Maps and search for your school. Have any parents or community members left "reviews" about your school? How is your school portrayed on Google Maps?

4. Your next stop is Foursquare, a geotagging website that allows people to "check in" to places and become the "mayor" of a business on their site. Search for your school at Foursquare and see if any parents, students, or teachers have "checked in" to your school.

5. Last but not least, take a trip to Wikipedia and search for your school. Is the information here accurate? How is your school portrayed on Wikipedia, the largest and most well-known encyclopedia on the web?

These are just a few of the social networking possibilities that current parents and prospective parents and students can use to better understand what your school is about.

ARE YOU AVAILABLE OR INVISIBLE?

The phone book of this century is digital and the websites noted in the next section are just some of the entries for your school in this new digital phone book. These are the places that people come to today to see what your school is about. The billboard out front is a start, but no longer is it the main communication vehicle to your parents and students.

If you're reading this chapter right now with a smile on your face because your school isn't present on any or some of the spaces discussed, think again. The absence of your students' and parents' work, thoughts, and suggestions says as much as a middle-of-the-road online profile. Think of the reaction you might have to three books on Amazon.com—one with five stars but costing $50, the other with three stars and slightly off topic but costing $10, and one at $12 with the right subject but no reviews. The fact is, if you're like most people, you'll probably not even dip deeper into the $12 book's description, instead making a choice between an expensive and well-reviewed or slightly off-topic, mediocre, but on-price tome. With more schools and states allowing open transfers and enrollments to schools, today what the Internet does not say about your school could be just as harmful as what it does.

There is no one single place that a school can be; it must exist in many spaces simultaneously. The following resources will help get you and your school started in taking control of your social network presence.

Additional Resources for Creating Your School's Online Profile

Six Spaces of Social Media: http://test.org .uk/2007/08/10/six-spaces-of-social-media/

Schools Take Control or Forfeit Your Profile: www.thethinking stick.com/schools-take-control-or-forfeit-your-profile

Taking Control of Your School's Profile: Where to Start: www.thethinkingstick.com/taking-control-of-your-schools-profile-where-to-start

WHERE TO START IN TAKING CONTROL

So where do you start to build your school's digital profile as a school leader? You start where your community is, which means having conversations with students and parents of your school to find out which social networks they use and if they would feel comfortable having the school use those social networks to stay in contact. Facebook and YouTube are great starting points but there are many social networks out there and your school community might be using something different. This conversation also needs to be ongoing. Social networking environments are moving very quickly. One day everyone is on Myspace, the next they are on Facebook. Who knows what the next social network might be or when it might come along? Keeping lines of communication open with your community is vital to know where you need to be as a school to take control of your school's digital profile.

One suggestion is to hire a social network community manager. The position is new to schools but has been around in the business industry for many years now. Trying to control all of these networks while doing a day-to-day job is almost impossible. A quick search on Google will find you some great job descriptions that you can use to create the position within your school or district or maybe a teacher at your school would be willing to take on the job.

How you go about taking control of social networks and using them to interact with your wider school community is not as important as when to start. The longer schools wait to get on board, the more ground school leaders will have to make up.

References

Churchill, C. (2010, March 2). Facebook could be parent-teacher link. *The Herald*. Retrieved from www.heraldscotland .com/news/education/facebook-could-be-parent-teacher-link-1.1010525#have-your-say

Countries with top Facebook penetration to population. (2010, November 3). Socialbakers. Retrieved from http://www.face bakers.com/blog/25-countries-with-top-facebook-penetration-to-population/?cacheDisable=1

Godula, G., Li, D., & Yu, R. (2009, April 5). *Chinese social networks "virtually" out-earn Facebook and MySpace: A market analysis.* TechCrunch. Retrieved from http://techcrunch.com/2009/04/05/chinese-social-networks-virtually-out-earn-facebook-and-myspace-a-market-analysis/

Lardinois, F. (2010, September 30). *Facebook is now the second largest video site in the U.S.* ReadWriteWeb. Retrieved from www .readwriteweb.com/archives/facebook_is_now_the_second_largest_video_site_after_youtube.php

Older users becoming dominant on Facebook. (n.d.). guardian.co.uk. Retrieved from www.guardian.co.uk/technology/blog/2009/jul/07/facebook-socialnetworking

scho, D. (n.d.). *1st grade Facebook*. Retrieved from http://prezi .com/1i2xbmaorrzq/1st-grade-facebook/

Social networks now more popular than search engines in the UK. (2010, June 8). Experian Hitwise. Retrieved from http://weblogs.hitwise .com/robin-goad/2010/06/social_networks_overtake_search_ engines.html?utm_source=feedburner&utm_medium=feed&utm_ campaign=Feed:+hitwise+%28Hitwise+Intelligence%29

Wikipedia. (2011). *Orkut.* Retrieved from http://en.wikipedia .org/wiki/Orkut

AFTERWORD

Christopher D. Sessums

Many instructional and educational technologists make integrating technology effectively into the classroom sound so easy, so seductive. They point to charts and data that show the concentration of technology in the hands of teenagers and adults as if they could ensure that all the parts will work together seamlessly and effectively. The reality is that from the ground many schools look like giant dysfunctional families whose members don't speak to each other and pursue their own short-term agendas despite district initiatives and state standards, and technology alone can't change this situation. This book represents a chance for educational leaders to learn about the changes afforded by a host of digital tools and applications from people who are taking a lead role in integrating technology in education. As an educational leader, your willingness to read this book with your reasonable doubts and anxieties in hand suggests an acknowledgment of the importance of the role that technology and ordinary people can play by driving this process. If you feel that the education industry in recent years has seemed at odds with its stakeholders—trying to force teachers, students, and parents into new relationships while still following established norms—feel free to use this book to justify your decisions to think differently.

You can scarcely blame teachers for not knowing how to speak this new language or even what questions to ask when so little effort is made to educate them about effectively integrating technology into the classroom. School districts and states often have ambitious plans yet fundamentally different business models and visions than local schools, principals, parents, and students.

Currently, the most-used computer program in schools is PowerPoint. What do we learn about computing and critical thinking by knowing how to create a PowerPoint presentation? The answer is nothing. It certainly doesn't teach you how to think critically.

All can agree that the core challenge is to expand the use of technology to support teaching and learning opportunities. What are our children and teachers going to do with computers in school? What are they going to do with them at home? We have the technology to bring about cultural and social changes in the way we think, learn, play, work, share, and collaborate, but as institutions schools have yet to figure out how to make this happen in a safe, effective, and meaningful way.

MIT professor Sherry Turkle noted that computers are both seductive and appealing. Clearly, there's little harm in using their seductive and appealing power to draw people in, to get people using them, and to begin a conversation. The important question is, "What happens after that?" In an interview transcribed on the PBS Digital Nation website (2010), Turkle articulated an important moment in our fascination with technology in education: "People talking about computers in education for the most part [are] talking about children using computer tools. They're not talking about understanding this technology."

Not understanding the technology is problematic on many levels. Many of us do not understand the layers of programming and thought that drives the applications and interfaces that we use. Because most of us are not programmers, we must settle for what others create as opposed to creating tools and applications that may be more appropriate or fit us better. Think of PowerPoint or Microsoft Word offering suggestions for correcting our grammar and spellings: "PowerPoint does more than provide a way of transmitting content. It carries its own way of thinking, its own aesthetic—which not surprisingly shows up in the aesthetic of college freshmen. In that aesthetic, presentation becomes its own powerful idea" (Turkle, 2004).

Aesthetic, the *form*, becomes confused with the *function*, the work itself. We have yet to look beyond the surface of technology; we have yet to reconcile a reflection of the moon with the actual thing itself. In school we teach kids to use these tools and not necessarily to understand what technology affords and what we gain and lose from using it.

This is not to say that every child needs to be trained in how to design microprocessors. But it does suggest that every child should be trained how to understand and write simple computer programs—that all programs can be changed and adjusted to meet specific needs. This is a level of critical thinking that we can easily be fostering in schools through use of the various applications discussed in this book. New digital media requires a deeper examination of the value we have given it. As Turkle wisely suggests, "Technology makes certain things easy educationally in the classroom. That doesn't necessarily mean that those things are the most educationally valuable" (Turkle, 2004).

Using technology to explore ideas that cannot fit within the prescribed school day means taking all participants out of their comfort zones. Working with administrators, community leaders, parents, teachers, and students is challenging and difficult to sustain because the time spans, design, development, integration, and assessment vary for all involved. Should teachers be developing content that is critical at a local level and should it match that which is required at the district and state level? What level of input should parents and community members have? Does this input match district and state standards? What is the most effective way to balance these forces? What role should assessment play in all of this? When will teachers be given time to innovate? What level of support will they have?

In many cases, what schools are failing to provide are positive relationships between students and mentors. Technology is certainly seductive and a wonderful place to begin learning, but it can never replace relationships between people who care. Focusing on using computers to support productive, meaningful collaborations is essential if we expect computing in education to hold real value. The hard job of education is getting kids to love and value learning. In what ways can we use technology and mentoring relationships to assist kids in finding something in learning that fits with their life and experiences and can lead to better lives ahead? As many of the chapters in this book illustrate (see, for example, the chapters on blogs, wikis, and social networking), interactivity and collaboration are not ends in and of themselves. They are a means to an end that isn't always rosy and perfect.

So, who controls the future of education? Every path forward has roadblocks, most of which feel insurmountable. Somehow these impediments will either have to be routed around or broken down in the coming decades. Borrowing from Henry Jenkins's (2006) work on participatory culture, the messages are clear:

- Technology is here and we need to be prepared to integrate it effectively into the curricula.
- Technology integration is harder than it sounds.
- Everyone will survive and prosper if everyone works together.

Unfortunately, working together is the one thing nobody seems to know how to do well.

Once upon a time, schools taught subject matter and basic socialization skills and little else; their involvement with technology and media was slight. Each subject had its own distinctive teachers and foci, and each was regulated under a particular set of standards and skills, depending on its perceived value to society. These differences were largely the product of political choices and preserved through habit rather than any essential characteristic of the various technologies that support their use. Central control was the norm due to the increased growth and demand for formal education.

Today, several forces have begun to break down the walls separating technology and content knowledge. New media and digital technologies enable the same content to flow through many different channels and assume many different forms. We are currently in a prolonged transition in which various technologies compete and collaborate in search of stability that seems to always be beyond our reach. For many educational leaders, the question of technology integration involves determining how to maintain the potential for knowledge growth and new digital media integration in the wake of high-stakes testing and economic instability.

New instructional technologies and digital media such as the ones identified in this book do not necessarily lead to stability or unity. They may be employed as a means to generate new knowledge and the presentation of knowledge, but they will always work within a system of dynamic tension and change.

This book describes for school leaders some of the ways that new digital media is reshaping education in the twenty-first century and the relationship between students and teachers as consumers and creators of content knowledge. None of the authors are neutral observers. We are all active participants in new digital media exploration. We are not merely consumers of new digital media, we also are creators. It is our business to show others what we've learned and to offer new perspectives on how these new tools might be used to support teaching and learning. New digital media does not replace older classroom media. Instead, their status and functions are shifted by the introduction of newer technologies.

As we look to the immediate future, new digital media will continue to be a mishmash of different technologies and strategies. The cultural shifts brought about by these technologies; the legal, privacy, and safety concerns; and the economic considerations all are preceding shifts in technological infrastructures that support these new media in schools and society. How these transitions play out will have a great impact on how technology is integrated in schools. Consequently, it is important for all of us to consider the human and educational purposes being served by technology integration. The chapters in this book, we hope, will help leaders better facilitate powerful learning and teaching with digital technologies in their school organizations.

References

digital_nation: Life on the virtual frontier. (2010, February 2). Interview with Sherry Turkle. Retrieved from www.pbs.org/wgbh/pages/frontline/digitalnation/interviews/turkle.html?utm_campaign=videoplayer&utm_medium=fullplayer&utm_source=relatedlink

Jenkins, H. (2006). *Convergence culture: Where old and new media collide*. New York: New York University Press.

Turkle, S. (2004, January). How computers change the way we think. *The Chronicle Review*. Retrieved from http://chronicle.com/article/How-Computers-Change-the-Way/10192

ABOUT THE EDITORS

Scott McLeod

http://dangerouslyirrelevant.org and http://minddump.org
• http://twitter.com/mcleod • dr.scott.mcleod@gmail.com

Scott McLeod's love of technology may stem from watching all those television episodes of *Ultraman*, *Speed Racer*, and *The Jetsons* when he was a kid. An associate professor of educational leadership at the University of Kentucky in Lexington, Kentucky, he also is the director of the UCEA Center for the Advanced Study of Technology Leadership in Education (CASTLE), the nation's only academic center dedicated to the technology needs of school administrators, and was a co-creator of the wildly popular video series, *Did You Know? (Shift Happens)*. He has received multiple awards for his technology leadership work, including recognition from the cable industry, Phi Delta Kappa, and the National School Boards Association. Scott blogs regularly about technology leadership issues at *Dangerously Irrelevant* and *Mind Dump* and occasionally at *The Huffington Post*.

Chris Lehmann

http://practicaltheory.org • http://twitter.com/chrislehmann
• chris@practicaltheory.org

Chris Lehmann is the founding principal of the Science Leadership Academy (SLA), a joint venture between the Franklin Institute and the School District of Philadelphia. SLA has been recognized as an Apple Distinguished School and was named one of the "Ten Most Amazing Schools" by *Ladies Home Journal* in 2010. Among his many honors, Chris was named one of the "30 Most Influential People in EdTech" by *Tech & Learning* magazine in 2010. He has shared his vision with educators all over the country. Chris is the author of the education blog *Practical Theory* and is father to Jakob and Theo.

ABOUT THE CONTRIBUTORS

Carl Anderson

http://carlanderson.blogspot.com • http://twitter.com/anderscj
• anderscj@yahoo.com

Carl Anderson is a technology integration specialist and art teacher
in Rochester, Minnesota. He is an adjunct instructor for Hamline
University and an online 7–12 art and technology teacher for
Minnesota Connections Academy. He also is a technology integration consultant and has worked with many traditional public,
magnet, and charter schools in the state of Minnesota.

Michael Barbour

www.michaelbarbour.com • http://twitter.com/mkbwsu
• mkbarbour@gmail.com

Michael Barbour is an assistant professor at Wayne State University
in Detroit, Michigan, where he teaches instructional technology
and qualitative research methodology. Originally from the
largely rural Canadian province of Newfoundland and Labrador,
Michael's current research interests focus on the effective design,
delivery, and support of online learning to K–12 students in virtual
school environments, particularly those in rural jurisdictions.

Richard Byrne

http://freetech4teachers.com • http://twitter.com/rmbyrne
• richardbyrne@freetech4teachers.com

Richard Byrne is a high school social studies teacher in South Paris,
Maine. Named in 2010 as one of the "30 Leaders of the Future in
EdTech" by *Technology & Learning Magazine*, Richard writes the
award-winning blog, *Free Technology for Teachers*.

Kimberly Cofino

http://kimcofino.com/blog • http://twitter.com/mscofino
• mscofino@gmail.com

Originally from the United States, Kimberly Cofino is an enthusiastic and innovative globally minded educator. Kim has been teaching internationally for over ten years: in Munich, Germany; in Kuala Lumpur, Malaysia; in Bangkok, Thailand; and now as technology and learning coach at Yokohama International School in Japan. As an Apple Distinguished Educator, her work focuses on helping core subject teachers authentically embed current and emerging technologies in the classroom to create global and collaborative learning environments.

Alec Couros

http://couros.ca • http://twitter.com/courosa • couros@gmail.com

Alec Couros is a professor of educational technology and media for the Faculty of Education, University of Regina, in Saskatchewan, Canada. His graduate and undergraduate courses help teachers and teacher candidates better use the educational potential afforded by tools of connectivity.

Vicki A. Davis

http://coolcatteacher.blogspot.com • http://twitter.com/
coolcatteacher • vicki@coolcatteacher.com

Vicki A. Davis is a leading educational blogger located in the small town of Camilla, Georgia, where she teaches technology courses in grades 8–12 and serves as IT director. As the cofounder of the internationally recognized *Flat Classroom*, *Digiteen*, *NetGenEd*, and *Eracism* projects, Vicki coordinates thousands of students per year who are using wikis as collaborative learning tools. She blogs at the *Cool Cat Teacher* blog.

Steve Dembo

http://teach42.com • http://twitter.com/teach42
• sdembo@gmail.com

A former kindergarten teacher and school director of technology, Steve Dembo is a pioneer in the field of educational social networking. Among the first educators to realize the power of blogging, podcasting, Twitter, and other Web 2.0 technologies to connect educators to one another and create professional learning communities, Steve has been instrumental in the explosive growth of the Discovery Educator Network. Steve lives in Skokie, Illinois.

Richard E. Ferdig

www.ferdig.com • rferdig@gmail.com

Richard E. Ferdig is the RCET Research Professor and professor of instructional technology at Kent State University in Kent, Ohio. He works within the Research Center for Educational Technology and also the School of Lifespan Development and Educational Sciences. Rick earned his PhD in educational psychology from Michigan State University. At Kent State, his research, teaching, and service focus on combining cutting-edge technologies with current pedagogic theory to create innovative learning environments.

Karl Fisch

http://thefischbowl.blogspot.com • http://twitter.com/karlfisch • karlfisch@gmail.com

Karl Fisch has taught middle and high school math for twenty-one years, is the director of technology at Arapahoe High School in Centennial, Colorado, and is the original creator of the *Did You Know? (Shift Happens)* series of videos that has helped start millions of conversations about education all around the world. Karl has been named one of the National School Board Association's "20 to Watch," the "Outstanding Leader of the Year" by the International Society for Technology in Education, one of the "30 Leaders of the Future in EdTech" by *Technology & Learning Magazine*, and one of the fifteen "Featured Doers" in *The Huffington Post*'s Spotlight

Series on innovation. He invites you to join the conversation on his blog, *The Fischbowl*.

Scott S. Floyd
http://scottsfloyd.com • http://twitter.com/woscholar
• floyds@woisd.net

After ten years in the classroom, mostly teaching middle school reading, English, and gifted and talented courses, Scott S. Floyd currently serves as the technology curriculum specialist for the White Oak Independent School District in White Oak, Texas. His focus is on helping teachers integrate technology tools into their curriculum when appropriate for both instruction and personal learning.

Wesley Fryer
www.speedofcreativity.org • http://twitter.com/wfryer
• wesfryer@yahoo.com

Based in Edmond, Oklahoma, Wesley Fryer is an international learning consultant, author, digital storyteller, educator, and change agent. With respect to school change, he describes himself as a "catalyst for creative engagement and collaborative learning." Wesley is the executive director of the nonprofit Story Chasers, Inc., the lead partner in the *Celebrate Oklahoma Voices* and *Celebrate Kansas Voices* digital storytelling projects.

Miguel Guhlin
http://mguhlin.net • http://twitter.com/mguhlin
• mguhlin@gmail.com

Miguel Guhlin is the director of instructional technology for the San Antonio Independent School District in San Antonio, Texas. A published author and accomplished speaker with twenty years of professional development facilitation, Miguel works to enhance collaboration in transforming teaching, learning, and leading through the strategic application of technology. Envisioning

solutions to problems at the cusp of transformation fascinates him
and those he serves.

Mary Beth Hertz
http://philly-teacher.blogspot.com • http://twitter.com/mbteach
• marybethhertz@gmail.com

Mary Beth Hertz is a technology teacher and technology integration specialist at a small K–6 elementary school in Philadelphia,
Pennsylvania. She writes the elementary technology integration
blog for *Edutopia*, has presented at numerous conferences, is one of
the organizers of Edcamp Philly, and moderates the weekly #edchat
Twitter chat.

Tom Hoffman
http://tuttlesvc.org • http://twitter.com/tuttle_svc
• tom.hoffman@gmail.com

Tom Hoffman is project manager of *SchoolTool*, an open source
student information system for the developing world, funded by
Mark Shuttleworth. Tom has a master's in teaching from Brown
University and is a former English teacher and technology coordinator in the Providence (Rhode Island) Public School District.

Kristin Hokanson
http://khokanson.net • http://twitter.com/khokanson
• kristin.hokanson@gmail.com

Kristin Hokanson is a technology integrator and classroom teacher
at Upper Merion High School outside Philadelphia, Pennsylvania.
As an affiliated faculty member with the Media Education Lab
at Temple University and regional director of the Pennsylvania
Association for Educational Communications and Technology,
Kristin strives to help teachers to develop a greater understanding of media literacy and responsibility in an increasingly digital
society.

David Jakes

www.jakesonline.org • http://twitter.com/djakes
• dsjakes@gmail.com

David Jakes has been a teacher, administrator, and staff developer for twenty-five years. He currently serves Glenbrook South High School in Glenview, Illinois, as instructional technology coordinator.

Kevin Jarrett

www.ncs-tech.org • http://twitter.com/kjarrett
• kevin_jarrett@yahoo.com

Kevin Jarrett teaches in the K–4 Computer Lab at Northfield Elementary School in Northfield, New Jersey, where he has worked since 2003. He is a second-career educator (he left a high-paying position in the corporate world after September 11) and a passionate, lifelong learner committed to transforming teaching and learning through technology.

Doug Johnson

www.doug-johnson.com • http://twitter.com/blueskunkblog
• doug0077@gmail.com

Doug Johnson is the director of media and technology for the Mankato Public Schools in Mankato, Minnesota. His teaching experience has included work in grades K–12. He is the author of five books, a long-running column in *Library Media Connection*, the *Blue Skunk Blog*, and articles in more than forty books and periodicals. Doug has worked with more than 130 organizations around the world and has held leadership positions in state and national organizations, including the International Society for Technology and Education and the American Association of School Librarians.

Liz Kolb

http://cellphonesinlearning.com • http://twitter.com/lkolb
• elikeren@umich.edu

Liz Kolb is a lecturer and research associate at the University of Michigan in Ann Arbor, where she instructs and coordinates the education technology teacher education program. She received her PhD in learning technologies from the University of Michigan. She is a former high school social studies teacher and technology coordinator.

Diana Laufenberg

http://laufenberg.wordpress.com • http://twitter.com/dlaufenberg • dlaufenberg@gmail.com

Diana Laufenberg currently works with eleventh- and twelfth-grade students at the Science Leadership Academy in Philadelphia. Experiential education is an integral part of her educational pursuits, taking students from the classroom to the real world and back again. Before finding her way to Philadelphia, she was an active member of the teaching community in Flagstaff, Arizona, where she was named the Arizona "Technology Teacher of the Year" and a member of the Governor's Master Teacher Corps.

Pamela Livingston

www.1-to-1learning.blogspot.com • http://twitter.com/plivings • pamelajlivingston@gmail.com

Pamela Livingston is the author of the book, *1-to-1 Learning: Laptop Programs That Work*; writes articles for educational technology journals and magazines; and frequently presents workshops and keynotes in the United States and internationally. An adjunct professor at Chestnut Hill College in Philadelphia, Pamela has directed technology at independent, charter, and public schools in the United States. Currently the senior collaborator for *Educational Collaborators*, she helps schools plan, implement, and evaluate one-to-one laptop programs.

Christian Long

http://beplayfuldesign.com and http://prototypedesigncamp.com • http://twitter.com/christianlong • christian@beplayfuldesign.com

Based in Worthington, Ohio, Christian Long is a school planner, technology expert, passionate advocate for innovative learning communities, and educator. Christian is the founder of Be Playful, a collaborative global design agency focused on the intersection among school planning and design, emerging technology, professional development, and future trending. He also is the founder of *Prototype Design Camp*, an innovative design program for young creatives collaborating on real-world problems. Additionally, Christian speaks nationally and internationally on topics ranging from emerging trends in education, twenty-first-century technology and social media, and innovative school planning practices.

Ewan McIntosh
www.ewanmcintosh.com • http://twitter.com/ewanmcintosh
• ewan@ewanmcintosh.com

Ewan McIntosh is an award-winning teacher, speaker, and investor regarded as one of Europe's foremost experts in digital media for public services. A resident of Edinburgh, Ewan was Scotland's first National Advisor on Learning and Technology Futures and now takes the most creative practices from the world of technology, film, and television back to education.

Mathew Needleman
www.videointheclassroom.com • http://twitter.com/mrneedleman
• mrneedleman@gmail.com

Mathew Needleman, a teacher, filmmaker, and literacy coach in Culver City, California, has been integrating digital filmmaking into elementary classrooms for thirteen years. He holds a master's degree in educational leadership and policy and is an Apple Distinguished Educator.

Sheryl Nussbaum-Beach
http://21stcenturycollaborative.com and http://plpnetwork.com
• http://twitter.com/snbeach • sherylnbeach@gmail.com

Sheryl Nussbaum-Beach is a twenty-year educator who has been a classroom teacher, technology coach, charter school principal, district administrator, university instructor, and digital learning consultant. A doctoral candidate at the College of William & Mary in Williamsburg, Virginia, she is a noted international keynote speaker and cofounder of the Powerful Learning Practice Network. Sheryl blogs at www.21stcenturycollaborative.com.

John W. Rice

http://edugamesresearch.com/blog • http://twitter.com/
• j7r7@hotmail.com

John W. Rice serves as the director of technology for a school district near Bryan, Texas. Also a doctoral student, John's research interests relate to instructional video games and he maintains a blog devoted to the topic at www.edugamesresearch.com.

Will Richardson

www.weblogg-ed.com and http://plpnetwork.com • http://twitter
.com/willrich45 • will@plpnetwork.com

Will Richardson is a parent, author, blogger, speaker, and former public school educator who has spent the better part of the last seven years helping educators understand the changes that the web is bringing to learning and to schools. He is the cofounder of the Powerful Learning Practice Network, which has provided long-term, job-embedded professional development to thousands of educators around the world, and is a national advisory board member for the George Lucas Education Foundation. A resident of Flemington, New Jersey, Will also is the author of *Blogs, Wikis, Podcasts and Other Powerful Web Tools for the Classroom*, Corwin Press's "Book of the Year" in 2008, and is a regular columnist for *District Administration* magazine.

Stephanie Sandifer

http://ed421.com • http://twitter.com/ssandife
• stephaniedsandifer@gmail.com

Stephanie Sandifer is an educator with nearly twenty years of experience educating children and adults at all levels. As a K–12 and college-level educator, Stephanie has over fifteen years of experience in the classroom—in face-to-face and virtual school settings—and ten years of experience in leadership roles that encompass a wide range of school administration, curriculum, instruction, and professional development responsibilities. Stephanie lives in Houston, Texas, and works from home as an online educator, author, professional development provider, and consultant.

Christopher D. Sessums
www.csessums.com • http://twitter.com/csessums
• csessums@gmail.com

Christopher D. Sessums is a postdoctoral associate in educational technology in the School of Teaching and Learning at the University of Florida in Gainesville, Florida, where he teaches and conducts research on open learning and participatory media. Christopher has been teaching professionally since 1997 and is the former director of distance learning in the Office of Distance, Continuing, and Executive Education and in the College of Education at the University of Florida.

Dean Shareski
http://shareski.ca • http://twitter.com/shareski
• shareski@gmail.com

Dean Shareski is a digital learning consultant for Prairie South School Division in Saskatchewan, Canada. Dean has been blogging, sharing, and connecting online since 2005. In 2010 Dean was given the "Outstanding Leader" award by the International Society for Technology in Education.

Sharon Tonner
http://tecnoteacher.blogspot.com • http://twitter.com/tecnoteach
• s.a.tonner@dundee.ac.uk

A lecturer in primary education at the University of Dundee in Scotland, Sharon Tonner prepares primary-level student teachers for the classrooms of today and tomorrow, not yesterday. Her main research centers on using handheld technologies to enhance learning through personalization and interactivity.

Jeff Utecht
www.jeffutecht.com • http://twitter.com/jutecht
• jeff@jeffutecht.com

Currently in Bangkok, Thailand, Jeff Utecht is an international educator, educational technology consultant, and author. Over the past nine years, Jeff has taught in international schools in the Middle East and Asia. From camels and cell phones in the deserts of Saudi Arabia to the twenty-first-century city of Shanghai, China, Jeff's travels have allowed him to experience technology and globalization through the lens of education.

Joyce Kasman Valenza
http://blog.schoollibraryjournal.com/neverendingsearch and http://springfieldlibrary.wikispaces.com • http://twitter.com/joycevalenza
• joycevalenza@gmail.com and joyce_valenza@sdst.org

Joyce Kasman Valenza is the teacher-librarian at Springfield Township High School in Erdenheim, Pennsylvania. She writes the *NeverEndingSearch* blog for *School Library Journal* and writes for a number of other library and educational technology publications. Joyce speaks nationally and internationally about the thoughtful use of technology in learning.

Mark Wagner
www.edtechteam.com/team/markwagner • http://twitter.com/markwagner • mark@edtechteam.com

Formerly a high school English teacher, Mark Wagner has since served as an educational technology coordinator at the site, district, and county levels. He now serves as president and CEO of the EdTechTeam, which provides professional development and consulting services to schools, districts, and other educational institutions, including Computer Using Educators (CUE). A resident of Irvine, California, Mark serves as the director of the Google Teacher Academy as part of his work for CUE.

David Warlick

http://2cents.davidwarlick.com • http://twitter.com/dwarlick • david.warlick@gmail.com

Based in Raleigh, North Carolina, David Warlick is an author, programmer, public speaker, and entrepreneur. He also is a thirty-four-year educator as a classroom teacher, administrator, and state department of education staff consultant. David has written four books, developed education websites that serve more than a million people a day, and spoken to audiences around the world.

INDEX